IN HIS
STEPS

by
Charles M. Sheldon

IN HIS STEPS

by
Charles M. Sheldon

Edited by James S. Bell Jr.

This Billy Graham Evangelistic Association special edition is published with permission from Honor Books.

Honor Books
Tulsa, Oklahoma

IN HIS STEPS:
A Timeless Classic Updated in Today's Language
Original novel copyright © 1897 by Charles M. Sheldon
ISBN 0-913367-15-X
Copyright © 1998 by Honor Books
P. O. Box 55388
Tulsa, Oklahoma 74155

Edited and introduced by James S. Bell Jr.
Development and writing by Paul M. Miller
Cover photo by Gary Johnson

EDITOR'S NOTE

Charles Sheldon could not have imagined the impact his series of sermons would have on the Christian world when he presented them to his church in Topeka, Kansas. He simply wanted to demonstrate in fictionalized form what might happen to a church and community if people began to walk in a way that would reflect what they felt Jesus would do if He were in their place. Yet, when this unique approach to Christian discipleship was published in 1897, it was an immediate bestseller, and now it is estimated that more than 15 million copies have been read during the past 100 years. Many of these readers have asked themselves what Jesus would do in countless situations, and we will never fully know how their changed lives have affected our world.

Much of Sheldon's story is autobiographical. A social reformer and an idealist, Sheldon strove to improve social conditions as part of ushering in the Kingdom of God. His appeal was not to the intellect, but rather, to the will and passions of those out to save the world. As pastor of Central Congregational Church of Topeka, he was ahead of his time—an evangelical who embraced the social gospel, that is, to reach the whole person for Christ. He crusaded for civil rights on behalf of African-

Americans and Jews. He fought the excesses of alcoholism and served as an activist for peace. He sought denominational reconciliation by pursuing agreement on evangelical essentials and social justice by linking the Gospel with social activism.

Like Dietrich Bonhoeffer of the twentieth century, Charles Sheldon believed the cost of discipleship is everything—vices, prejudices, comforts, and selfish interests. It implies a willingness to move radically against the grain and a refusal to compromise even in the little things. It means taking the humble, lowly road and reaching out, even living among, what Jesus describes as the least of these. Following in His steps may not be glamorous or self-enhancing but it is the surest way to intimately know the Savior and His priorities for a lost world.

Reverend Sheldon's message is every bit as relevant today as it was when the text was originally introduced; however, the application of that truth and the author's writing style can pose a formidable barrier for today's reader. For that reason, the text has been updated in the following manner:

- Sentence structure has been simplified.
- Dialogue has been made more conversational.

- Reverend Maxwell's character has been portrayed as more open and less aloof.

- Occupations that play an important role in the narrative have been updated.

- Certain social expectations have been modernized.

- Technologies that were unavailable at the time the original text was written have been introduced into the storyline when appropriate.

All in all, it has been our intention to enhance the powerful message this book delivers by introducing it delicately into the world in which we now live. In so doing, it is our hope that it will affect a new generation in the same way it has affected millions in the past. We wish to note, however, that each step has been taken with trepidation in an effort to preserve the presence and texture of this remarkable work.

The potential for world revival has perhaps never been greater than it is in our present time. Just as in Sheldon's day, the world needs to see the complete self-sacrificing love of Christ, not only in word but also in the lives of His disciples. *In His Steps* demonstrates how this can take place, one community at a time.

Whatever your purpose for reading *In His Steps*, it is hoped that you will better learn what it means to follow Jesus and do as He would do in every situation in your life. May you have the grace and courage to be obedient to His call.

James S. Bell Jr.
1998

CHAPTER 1

To this you were called, because Christ
suffered for you, leaving you an example, that
you should follow in his steps.
I Peter 2:21

It was Friday morning and the Reverend Henry Maxwell was trying to finish his Sunday morning sermon. He had been interrupted several times and was growing nervous as the morning wore on and his sermon slowly moved toward a satisfactory finish.

"Mary," he called to his wife, as he went upstairs after the last interruption, "if anyone else phones or comes to the door, please tell them I'm busy and can't be disturbed unless it is something very important."

"I would, Henry. But I'm going over to visit the preschool, and you'll have the house all to yourself."

The minister went up into his study and shut the door. In a few minutes, he heard his wife leave, and quietness settled over the house. With a sigh of relief, he began to write. His text was from 1 Peter 2:21: *To this you were called, because*

Christ suffered for you, leaving you an example, that you should follow in his steps.

In the first part of the sermon, Maxwell emphasized Jesus' personal sacrifice for our sins, calling attention to the fact of Jesus' suffering in His life as well as in His death. He went on to emphasize our redemption with illustrations from Jesus' life and teachings, showing how faith in Christ helped to save men because of the pattern or character of His life displayed for their imitation. He was now on the third and last point, the necessity of following Jesus' example in His sacrifice.

He had just written "Three Steps, What Are They?" and was about to list them in logical order when the doorbell rang.

Henry Maxwell continued at his desk with an annoyed frown. The bell rang again. He rose and walked to a window overlooking the front door. A shabbily dressed young man was standing on the steps.

"Looks like some homeless person," said the minister. "I suppose I'll have to go down and—"

He did not finish his sentence but went downstairs and opened the front door. There was a moment's hesitation as the two men stood facing each other, then the shabby-looking young man said, "I'm out of a job, sir, and thought you might be able to suggest something."

"Jobs are scarce—," replied the minister, "I don't know of anything." He began to shut the door slowly.

"Maybe you could give me some names—," continued the young man, nervously fingering a faded cap.

"I'm afraid I don't know of anything. You will have to excuse me," Maxwell apologized. "I am very busy this morning. I hope you find something soon. Sorry I can't give you a job here, but my wife and I don't need much help."

Reverend Henry Maxwell closed the door and heard the man walk down the steps. There was something about the dejected figure, so homeless and forsaken, that the frustrated minister could not help but hesitate in front of a hall window and watch the young man make his way down the sidewalk. Then he moved back up to his study, and with a sigh, returned to his writing. There were no more interruptions, so when his wife returned two hours later the sermon was finished, the notes gathered up, clipped together, and placed by his Bible in preparation for the Sunday morning service.

"The strangest thing happened at the pre-school this morning, Henry," said his wife while they were eating dinner. "As you know I went over with Lenore Brown for a visit. Well, just after the games, while the children were having a snack, the door opened and a young man came in. He seemed quite polite; he took his cap off and sat down near the door. He never said a word, just sat there watching the children. He was evidently a homeless person like those who live downtown. Well, Dorothy Wren and her assistant were frightened at first, but he seemed harmless enough. Then he simply slipped out while we weren't paying attention."

"Perhaps he was tired and wanted to rest somewhere. I believe the same man came by here."

"Oh? Well, our man was about thirty years old, I'd say."

"The same man," said Reverend Maxwell thoughtfully.

"Did you finish your sermon, Henry?" his wife asked after a pause.

"Yes, all done. This week has been unbelievable, what with sermons and. . . ."

"They'll be appreciated by an overflowing congregation—I hope," replied his wife smiling. "What's your morning sermon about?"

"Following Christ. I take up the theme of redemption through His sacrifice and example, and then, show what is needed to follow in Christ's steps."

"I am sure it will be good, but I hope it doesn't rain. We have had so many stormy Sundays lately."

"Yes, our attendance has been down. And we know all too well that people will not come out to church in bad weather." Henry sighed in anticipation of the numbers that would fail to appear weather or no weather.

Sunday morning dawned on the town of Raymond as one of those perfect days that sometimes come after long periods of wind and mud and rain. The air was clear and bracing, the sky was free from all threatening signs, and everyone in Pastor Maxwell's parish prepared for church. When he read the "Call to Worship" at eleven o'clock, the sanctuary was filled with an impressive congregation of Raymond's finest.

The members of the First Church of Raymond believed in having only the best music, and its choir this morning was a source of great inspiration. All the music was in keeping with the theme of the sermon, including the choir anthem, which was an elaborate arrangement of a familiar hymn,

> *Jesus, I my cross have taken,*
> *All to leave and follow Thee.*

Just before the sermon, soprano Rachel Winslow sang a solo, the well-known hymn,

> *Where He leads me I will follow,*
> *I'll go with Him, with Him, all the way.*

Rachel Winslow was beautiful as she stood behind the choir screen of carved oak, and a general rustle of expectation swept over the audience as she prepared to sing. Reverend Maxwell settled himself contentedly in his pulpit chair. Rachel Winslow's singing always inspired him and gave a lift to the service, making his delivery more impressive.

On that bright morning, the congregation was more deeply moved than ever by her outstanding performance. It seemed to the minister that something supernatural swept through the church, and he was startled by it. As he rose, however, and laid his sermon and his Bible on the pulpit, he lost his feeling of the unusual and quickly became absorbed in his sermon.

No one had ever accused Henry Maxwell of being a dull preacher. On the contrary, he had often been accused of being sensational; not in what he had to say so much as in his way of saying it. The members of First Church liked that. It gave their preacher and their parish a welcome distinction.

It was also true that the pastor of First Church loved to preach. He seldom exchanged pulpits, choosing instead to be before his own people each Sunday. It was an exhilarating half hour as he faced a full sanctuary, knowing that he had a hearing. He was sensitive indeed to variations in the attendance, and never preached well before a small audience. He was at his best before an audience like the one he now faced, and he felt a glow of satisfaction. His church was the first in the city. It had the best choir, and was composed of the most influential people in Raymond. He took great pride in the circumstances of his pastorate and the influence his congregation wielded in the city. As he moved into his sermon, he felt a strong sense of confidence.

A deep sense of personal satisfaction over-whelmed Reverend Maxwell as he drew near the end of his message. He was certain he had communicated with his congregation. The sermon was interesting, filled with striking sentences, delivered dramatically and in good taste.

If Reverend Maxwell felt satisfied with the conditions of his pastorate, the members of First Church were equally content. They reveled in his scholarly, refined, somewhat striking face and figure and his ability to preach with passion and free of any irritating mannerisms.

Suddenly, in the midst of this feel-good atmosphere between minister and congregation, a remarkable incident occurred. It was so unexpected, so entirely beyond any thought of any person present that it offered no room for argument or, for the time being, resistance.

The sermon had come to a close, and Reverend Maxwell had just turned the other half of the big Bible over onto his written sermon and was about to sit down as the quartet prepared to sing the closing selection,

All for Jesus, all for Jesus,
All my being's ransomed powers,

when the entire congregation was startled by the sound of a man's voice. It came from the rear of the church, from one of the seats under the balcony. The next moment, a man emerged from the shadows and walked down the middle aisle. Before the startled congregation could understand what was happening, the man reached the open space in front of the pulpit and turned to face them.

"I've been wondering since I came in here"— they were the words he used under the balcony and he repeated them—"if it would be all right for me to say a word at the close of the service. I'm not drunk or crazy, and I am perfectly harmless, but if I die, as there is every likelihood I will in a few days, I would like to think that I had my say in a place like this and before the kind of people who are gathered here today."

Reverend Maxwell had not taken his seat, and he now remained standing, leaning against his pulpit, looking down at the stranger. It was the man who had come to his house the Friday before, the same dusty, worn, shabby-looking young man. As before, he held his faded hat in his hands, which seemed to be his favorite pose. He had not shaved and his hair was rough and tangled. Though the members of First Church had encountered such individuals out on the streets of downtown, no one like this had ever confronted them within the bounds of their own sanctuary. They never dreamed such a thing could happen.

There was nothing offensive in the man's manner or tone. He did not appear to be overly excited, and he spoke in a low but distinct voice. Reverend Maxwell was conscious, even as he stood there struck dumb with astonishment, that the man's action reminded him of a person who was walking and talking in his sleep.

No one made any motion to stop the stranger or in any way interrupt him. The shock of his sudden appearance had now deepened into a genuine uncertainty concerning how to best handle this unheard of situation. The young man continued to speak as if he had no thought of the incredibly odd nature of his presentation. And all the while, Reverend Maxwell leaned over the pulpit with his face growing whiter and sadder with each passing moment. Still, he made no movement to stop him. Rachel Winslow, from her seat in the choir, stared white-faced at the shabby figure with the faded hat.

"I'm not your ordinary street person," he said, "although I don't know of any teaching of Jesus that makes one homeless person less worthy of help than another. Do you?" He put the question as naturally as if he were speaking to a small group of friends. Then, he paused for a moment and coughed painfully.

"I am a printer by trade, but ten months ago, I lost my job. The new presses are beautiful, and I don't really blame the newspapers for wanting to use the most advanced equipment possible, but the reality is that many of us have lost our jobs as a result. What can a man do? I just learned one trade. I've walked all over this part of the country trying to find something. There are many others like me and few have had much success. I don't mean to complain, just state facts. As I sat there under the balcony though, I couldn't help wondering about something." The man turned about and looked up at the pulpit and then continued. "Your minister said that it is necessary for the disciple of Jesus to follow in His steps, and that the steps are obedience, faith, love, and imitation. But I did not hear him say what that means, especially the last step. What do you Christians mean by following in the steps of Jesus?

"I've walked all over this city for the past three days trying to find work, and in all that time, I haven't heard one word of sympathy or comfort except from your minister, who said he was sorry for me and hoped I would find a job soon. I suppose most people today are so bothered by professional panhandlers that they forget there are decent people who find themselves in this situation. I'm not blaming anyone; I just want to give you the facts. Of course, I understand you can't all go out of your way to find jobs for people like me, and I'm not asking you to. I'm just puzzled by what you mean when you say you are following Jesus. What do you mean when you sing 'I'll go with Him, with Him, all the way'? Do you mean that you are suffering and denying yourselves and trying to save lost, suffering humanity just as I understand Jesus did?

"Out there on the streets, I often see the ragged edge of things. I understand there are more than 500 homeless men and women in this city. And many of them have families. The shelters are overflowing. My wife died four months ago, and I'm glad her suffering has ended. My little girl is staying with friends until I find work. Perhaps that is why I feel confused when I see so many Christians living in luxury and singing 'Jesus, I my cross have taken, all to leave and follow Thee.' I keep remembering how my wife died in a tenement in New York City, gasping for air and asking God to help us. Of course I don't expect you people here to save every person who is dying from lack of proper nourishment or polluted air, but I do wonder what you specifically mean when you say you are following Jesus.

"Because, I was amazed to learn that a good many of the tenements in New York City are owned by Christian people. The owner of the building where my wife died is a member of a church. I can't help but wonder what it meant to him to follow Jesus all the way. The other night, I overheard some people singing,

> *All for Jesus, all for Jesus,*
> *All my being's ransomed powers,*
> *All my thoughts, and all my doings,*
> *All my days, and all my hours.*

and I kept wondering as I sat on the steps outside their church what they meant by the words of the song. It seems to me there's an awful lot of suffering in the world that wouldn't exist if all the people who sing such songs went out and lived them in the world. I suppose I don't understand. When you say you are following in Jesus' steps, do you mean you are determined to do what He would do?

"I can't help but notice that most of the people who attend these big churches wear expensive clothes and live in nice houses. They seem to have money to spend on luxuries and summer vacations, while thousands of people outside the churches walk the streets looking for work and eventually die in poverty. They survive with only the most meager of possessions and grow up in misery and hopelessness."

Suddenly, the man lurched in the direction of the communion table and laid one grimy hand on it. His hat fell onto the carpet at his feet and a stir went through the congregation. Dr. West half rose from his pew, but still the silence was unbroken by any voice or movement worth mentioning in the audience. The man put his other hand over his eyes, and then without any warning, fell heavily forward on his face, flat across the aisle. As he dashed down the pulpit steps, Henry Maxwell quickly said, "We will consider the service closed," and then knelt by the unconscious man. The audience instantly rose and filled the aisles, as Dr. West examined the man and announced that he was not dead, but had apparently fainted. "Probably heart trouble," the doctor muttered as he helped carry the man into the pastor's study.

CHAPTER 2

Reverend Maxwell and a group of his church members remained in the study for some time, watching over the man as he lay on the sofa breathing heavily. Dr. West had called the paramedics, who arrived quickly and confirmed his feeling that the man should be hospitalized immediately. However, the stranger refused to go and perhaps because he was indigent, Dr. West was able to take responsibility for his treatment. It was decided that the man would be moved to the parsonage, which was nearby and had an extra room.

"Mother has no company at present. I—I'm sure we could give this poor man a place to stay," Rachel Winslow offered.

She looked very agitated, but no one particularly noticed. They were all preoccupied with the strange event that had just taken place. It was the strangest situation that the members of First Church could ever remember. Reverend Maxwell thanked Rachel, but insisted on taking the man to his own home. Someone brought the car around and the ailing stranger was helped out of the church and a few minutes later, into the minister's spare room. Thus began a new chapter in Reverend Maxwell's life, bringing with it a permanent change in his definition of Christian discipleship.

The event created a great sensation in the First Church family. People talked of nothing else for a week. It was generally believed that the man had wandered into the church in a state of mental confusion. That seemed to be the only rational explanation for the man's actions. Members of the congregation were in agreement that the man had not spoken out of bitterness. His words had been mild and apologetic, almost as if he were one of their own seeking light on a very difficult subject.

On the third day, the man took a turn for the worse. A second doctor was brought in to examine him, but offered no hope. Hospitalization was once again considered, but the young man wanted desperately to spend his last days there in Reverend Maxwell's home. Since the doctors agreed that moving the man would not change his prognosis, he was allowed to remain. A full-time nurse would tend him around the clock and both doctors would drop by to check on his condition each day.

The young man's condition deteriorated as the week drew to a close, but he lingered through the following Saturday. On Sunday morning, just before one o'clock, he rallied and asked to see his child one last time. Reverend Maxwell had sent for her immediately after finding a name and address on a scrap of paper in the man's shirt pocket. Unfortunately, the man had been conscious and able to talk coherently only occasionally since his collapse.

"She'll be here in just a moment," Reverend Maxwell said after calling down to his wife and asking her to bring the child up. He then sat down in a chair near the bed. His face showed the strain of the week's vigil, for he had insisted on sitting up nearly every night.

"I will never see her again in this world," the man whispered. Then he uttered with great difficulty the words, "You have been good to me. Somehow I feel as if it was what Jesus would do."

A few minutes later, he turned his head slightly, and before Reverend Maxwell realized what was happening, the nurse said quietly, "He is gone."

The Sunday morning that dawned on the city of Raymond was exactly like the Sunday of a week before. Reverend Maxwell entered his pulpit to face one of the largest congregations that had ever crowded into the First Church. He was haggard and looked as if he had just risen from a long illness. His wife was at home with the little girl, who was struggling to deal with the recent death of both her parents. Reverend Maxwell felt a sense of relief that the man's troubles were over, and he remembered the man's gentle face as he opened his Bible on the pulpit as he had been doing for ten years.

No one could remember when Henry Maxwell had last preached without notes. He had done so occasionally when he was fresh out of seminary, but for a long time he had carefully written out every word of his morning sermon, and nearly always his evening message as well. His sermon that morning was neither striking nor impressive, and he spoke with considerable hesitation. It was evident that he was struggling to express some great idea. Near the close of the sermon, he seemed to gather a certain strength that had been painfully lacking at the beginning.

Finally, he closed his Bible and stepped out to the side of the pulpit. Facing his people, he began to talk to them about the remarkable scene of the week before.

"Our brother," somehow the words sounded a little strange coming from his lips, "passed away this morning. I have not yet learned much about him, except that he had one sister living in Chicago. As of this morning, we have been unable to reach her. His little girl will remain with us for the time being."

Reverend Maxwell paused and looked across the sanctuary. He thought he had never seen so many earnest faces during his entire pastorate. He was not yet able to share with his congregation concerning the crisis through which he was even now moving. But he did feel that they sensed something of what he was struggling to express concerning the message he carried in his heart.

So he went on.

"The appearance and words of the stranger who visited with us last Sunday have made a very powerful impression on me. I am not able to conceal from you or myself the fact that what he said, followed as it has been by his death in my home, has compelled me to ask as I never asked before, 'What does following Jesus really mean?' I am not ready to condemn any of us for what has happened. But that does not prevent me from feeling that what the man said here last Sunday was so true that we must face it straight on or admit our failure as Christian disciples. A good deal of what our guest said represents a challenge to the kind of Christianity that many of us experience.

"And I do not know that anytime is more appropriate than the present for me to propose a plan, which has been forming in my mind as a satisfactory reply to our young visitor's words."

Pastor Maxwell paused and looked into the faces of the strong and earnest men and women of First Church.

He could see Edward Norman, CEO of Norman Communications, a conglomerate that includes newspapers and television stations. He had been a member of First Church for ten years and no man was more honored in the community.

He could also see Alexander Powers, superintendent of production at the local steel mill. Sitting near the front, Reverend Maxwell spotted Donald Marsh, president of Lincoln College, situated in the suburbs of Raymond.

Milton Wright, one of Raymond's most successful merchants sat in the fifth row. He owned a number of malls and retail outlets scattered across the state. Nearby, he spotted Dr.

Charles West who, although still comparatively young, was chief of surgery at Memorial Hospital.

Jasper Chase, the author who had written one successful book and was said to be at work on a novel, looked up at him from a seat near the aisle. Also seated in the congregation was Miss Virginia Page, an heiress, who after the recent death of her father, had inherited a $10 million fortune. Virginia was also gifted with an unusually charming personality and intellect. And not least of all, Rachel Winslow, from her seat in the choir, glowed with her peculiar beauty this morning as she listened with intense interest.

The persons seated in the First Church congregation had always inspired an intense feeling of satisfaction in Reverend Maxwell. But, as he scanned their faces on this particular morning, he could not help but wonder how many of them would respond positively to the proposition he was about to make.

"What I am about to say should not seem unusual, yet I am aware what I am proposing may be so regarded by a number of the members of this church. But in order that we may have a thorough understanding of what we are considering, I will speak rather bluntly. I am asking for volunteers from the First Church who will pledge themselves, earnestly and honestly for an entire year, not to do anything without first asking the question, 'What would Jesus do?' Then after asking that question, I will expect each one to follow Jesus as exactly as he or she knows how, no matter what the result may be. I will of course include myself in this company of volunteers, and by the way, will determine to believe that my church family will not be surprised at my future conduct based upon this standard of action. I hasten to add that no one will oppose whatever is done if they think Christ would do it. Have I made my meaning clear?

"At the close of the service, I want all those who are willing to join this company to remain, and we will talk over the details of the plan. Our motto will be, 'What would Jesus do?' Our aim will be to act just as He would if He were here. Regardless of the nature of the results, we will aim to follow Jesus' steps as closely and as literally as we believe He taught His disciples to do. And those who volunteer to do this will pledge themselves to do it for an entire year, beginning today."

Henry Maxwell paused and looked out at his people. It is not easy to describe the sensation that such a simple proposition had apparently made. Men glanced at one another in astonishment. It was not like Reverend Maxwell to define Christian discipleship in this way. The proposition was understood well enough, but there was, apparently, a great difference of opinion as to the application of Jesus' teaching and example.

He calmly closed the service with a brief prayer. The organist began the postlude immediately after the benediction, and the people began to file out, engaging one another in conversation as they went. Animated groups stood throughout the sanctuary discussing their minister's plan. After several minutes, Reverend Maxwell asked that all those who had decided to remain go into the small chapel adjacent to the sanctuary. After greeting worshippers at the front door of the church, Reverend Maxwell finally returned to the sanctuary where he found the church empty. He walked over to the chapel and was startled to see the number of people who had stayed for the meeting. He had not made up his mind about any of his members, but he hardly expected that so many were ready to enter into such a literal testing of their Christian discipleship. There were perhaps fifty present, among them

Rachel Winslow and Virginia Page, Mr. Norman, President Marsh, Alexander Powers, Milton Wright, Dr. West, and Jasper Chase.

Closing the chapel door, he stood before this group of the faithful. His face was pale and his lips trembled with emotion. To him, this moment represented a genuine turning point in his own life as well as in the lives of his people. Until he or she is moved by the Holy Spirit, no person can tell what he or she might do or how the moment may change the current of a lifetime of fixed habits of thought and speech and action. Henry Maxwell did not yet know himself all that he would face, but he was aware of a great upheaval in his definition of Christian discipleship, and he was moved with a great depth of feeling as he looked into the faces of these people.

It seemed to him both fitting and appropriate to begin with a word of prayer. And so, he asked the assembled group to bow their heads and pray with him. As he prayed, Reverend Maxwell recognized that the room was filled with the presence of God. As the prayer continued, this presence grew in power. Everyone in the small chapel experienced it. The room was filled with His Spirit as plainly as if He had been visible.

When the prayer ended, there was a silence that lasted several moments. All heads were bowed, and Maxwell's face was wet with tears. Not one person present could have been more certain of God's divine blessing if an audible voice from heaven had sanctioned their pledge to follow the Master's steps. And so began the most serious movement ever started in the First Church of Raymond.

"We all understand," Maxwell said, speaking very quietly, "what we have undertaken to do. That is, we have pledged that we will make no decision in our daily lives without first asking the question, 'What would Jesus do?' regardless of the consequence to us. Sometime I shall be able to tell you about the marvelous change that has come over my life in the past week, but the experience I have been through since last Sunday has left me so dissatisfied with my previous definition of Christian discipleship that I have been compelled to take this action. I did not dare begin it alone. I know that I am being led by the hand of God's love in all this. The same divine impulse must have led you also.

"Once again, I want to be sure that we all understand fully what we have undertaken."

"I want to ask a question," said Rachel Winslow. Everyone turned toward her when she spoke. Her face glowed with a beauty that physical loveliness alone could not create.

"I am a little in doubt as to the source of our knowledge concerning what Jesus would do. Who is to decide for me just what He would do in my case? We live in a very different time than Jesus did. Each day we are confronted with perplexing issues that are not mentioned in the teachings of Jesus. How are we to know what He would do?"

"I don't have an answer," admitted Reverend Maxwell, "except that we will know as we study Jesus under the direction of the Holy Spirit. Remember what Christ said when He spoke to His disciples about the Holy Spirit in John 16:13-15, *But when he, the Spirit of truth, comes, he will guide you into all truth. He will not speak on his own; he will speak only what he hears, and he will tell you what is yet to come. He will bring glory to me by taking from what is mine and making it known to you. All that belongs to the Father is mine. That is why I said the Spirit will take from what is mine and make it known to you.* There is no other test that I know of. We shall all have to decide what Jesus would do after going to that source of knowledge."

"What if when we do certain things, others say to us, 'Jesus would not do that'?" someone asked.

"We can't prevent that. But we must be absolutely honest with ourselves. The standard of Christian action cannot vary in our behavior."

"And yet what one person thinks Jesus would do, another may refuse to accept as His probable course of action. What will make our conduct regularly Christlike? Will it be possible to reach the same conclusions always in all cases?" asked President Marsh.

Reverend Maxwell was silent for some time. Then he answered, "No, I don't believe we can expect that. But when it comes to a genuine, honest, enlightened effort to follow in Jesus' steps, I cannot believe there will be any confusion either in our own minds or in the judgment of others. We must be free from fanaticism on one hand and from too much caution on the other. If Jesus' example is to be our example, it certainly must be possible to follow it. But we need to remember this great fact. After we have asked the Spirit to tell us what Jesus would do and have received an answer, we are then obliged to act regardless of the consequences to ourselves. Is that understood?"

All the heads in the room nodded in agreement. The challenge was clear. They remained a few minutes longer, discussing details and asking questions. Then they agreed that a meeting would be held each week, at which time they would report the results of their quest to follow Jesus in this way. Henry Maxwell prayed again. And again as before the Spirit was present. Every head remained bowed a long time. Then they stood and left in silence. There was a feeling that went far beyond speech. The pastor silently shook hands with each of them as they went out. When the final worshipper was gone, Reverend Maxwell went into his study and remained there alone in prayer for nearly half an hour.

On the way home, Maxwell stopped by the mortuary and went into the room where the body of the young stranger lay. Looking into his face, he sought God again for strength and wisdom, not yet realizing that a movement had begun which would lead to the most remarkable series of events that the city of Raymond had ever known.

CHAPTER 3

Whoever claims to live in him
must walk as Jesus did.
1 John 2:6

Edward Norman, publisher of the Raymond Daily News, sat in his executive office on Monday morning and faced a new world. He had made his pledge to do nothing without first asking, "What would Jesus do?" in good faith. Besides a chain of newspapers, Norman's holdings also included three television stations in other states, all of which were under his new mode of operation—his pledge—in the small as well as the weighty issues of business and life. On this Monday morning, he confronted it with a degree of hesitation and a feeling close to fear.

Norman had come down to the office very early in order to have a few minutes alone before the members of his staff arrived. He sat at his desk with a growing thoughtfulness that became an unusual desire. He had yet to learn, with all the others in that little company who pledged to do the Christlike thing, that the Spirit of life was moving in power through his own life as never before. He rose and shut his door, and then did what he had not done for years. He knelt by his desk and prayed that God's divine presence and wisdom would direct him.

He rose with the day before him, and his promise clearly in his mind. "I'm ready for action," he seemed to say.

He opened his door and began to deal with the routines of the day. The managing editor had just come in and was seated at his desk in the adjoining room, and a reporter clicked away on a keyboard. Edward Norman stepped back into his office to write his weekly editorial observations from the CEO's point of view. All of the papers in his chain would carry the piece, and it was expected that his television station managers might pick it up for an editorial comment.

He had been writing for 15 minutes when the managing editor called out, "Here's the critic's review of that new foreign movie that wouldn't present itself for viewer rating. Todd and Barstow give it a five-star rave, even though it's pretty raunchy. It will make up more than a full column. I assume it all goes in? Should we run the promotional photo that came with the review as well?"

While Norman was not one of those corporate men who keeps an eye on every detail of his properties, the paper's managing editor often consulted his chief when he was in town. Sometimes, as in this case, it was merely a nominal inquiry.

"Yes—No. Let me see it."

He took the typewritten pages just as they had come from the wire service and read over them carefully. Then he laid the sheets down on his desk and did some very hard thinking.

"We won't run this," he said finally.

The managing editor was standing in the doorway between the two rooms. He was astounded at his chief's remark, and thought he had perhaps misunderstood him.

"What did you say?"

"Leave it out. We won't use it."

"But—" The managing editor was simply dumbfounded. He stared at Norman as if the man was out of his mind.

"I don't think, Clark, that it ought to be printed, and that's the end of it," said Norman, looking up from his desk.

Clark seldom had any words with the chief. His word had always been law in the office and he had seldom been known to change his mind. The circumstances now, however, seemed to be so extraordinary that Clark could not help expressing himself.

"Do you mean that the paper is to go to press without this review? The whole country's been awaiting the release of this film. The Paramount Theater is giving it a statewide premiere opening this weekend."

"I'm sorry for the theater, but yes. That's what I mean."

"But it's unheard of. All the other papers will print it. What will our subscribers say? Why, it is simply—," Clark paused, unable to find words to say what he thought.

Norman looked at Clark thoughtfully. His managing editor belonged to a church of a different denomination than Norman's. The two men had never discussed religious matters although he had been working for Norman for several years now.

"Come in here a minute, Clark, and shut the door," said Norman.

Clark came in and the two men faced each other alone. Norman did not speak for a minute. Then he said abruptly:

"Clark, if Christ was editor of a daily paper, do you honestly think He would print a positive review of this film? And provide a questionable photo with it?"

"No, I don't suppose He would."

"Well, that's my only reason for shutting this story out of the *News*. I'm sorry to override your authority, but I have decided not to do anything in connection with the papers or television stations for a whole year that I honestly believe Jesus would not do."

Clark could not have looked more amazed if the chief had suddenly gone crazy. In fact, he did think something was wrong, though Mr. Norman would be one of the last men in the world, in his judgment, to lose his mind.

"What effect will that have on the paper?" he finally managed to ask in a faint voice.

"What do you think?" asked Norman with a keen glance.

"I think your decision could potentially ruin the paper," replied Clark promptly. He was gathering up his bewildered senses, and continued, "Why, it isn't feasible to run a paper on such a basis. It's too idealistic. You would never be able to make a profit in today's world. Just as sure as you live, if you shut out this piece, you will lose thousands of subscribers. It doesn't take a prophet to see that. The most influential people in town are waiting for the release of this movie—they're eager to read it. They know it's opening tomorrow at the Paramount and we promised a spread on it. So when they get the paper this evening, they will expect half a page at least. Surely, we can't afford to disregard the wishes of the public to such an extent. In my opinion, that would be a great mistake."

Norman sat silent a minute. Then he spoke gently but firmly.

"Clark, what in your honest opinion is the right standard for determining conduct? Is the only right standard for everyone, the probable action of Jesus Christ? Would you say that the highest, best law for a man to live by is contained in asking the question, 'What would Jesus do?' And then doing it regardless of results? In other words, do you think people everywhere ought to follow Jesus' example as closely as they can in their daily lives?" Clark turned red, and moved uneasily in his chair before he answered the question.

"Why—yes—I suppose if you put it on the ground of what people ought to do there is no other standard of conduct. But the question is, what's feasible? Is it possible to make it work? To succeed in the newspaper or television industry, the desires of the general public must be considered. We aren't living in an ideal world."

"Do you mean that it's impossible to run a business strictly on Christian principles and make it succeed?"

"Yes, that's exactly what I mean. It can't be done. We'll go bankrupt in thirty days."

Norman did not reply at once. He was very thoughtful.

"We'll have an occasion to talk this over again, Clark. Meanwhile, I think we ought to understand each other frankly. I have pledged myself for a year to confront all of my decisions, whether for the papers or television stations, by answering the question, 'What would Jesus do?' as honestly as possible. I'll continue to do this, believing that not only will we succeed but that we will succeed to a greater degree than before."

Clark rose. "The review and the photo do not go in?"

"They do not. There is plenty of good material to present, and you know what it is."

Clark hesitated. "Are we going to say anything about the absence of the review and the premiere at the Paramount?"

"No, let the paper go to press as if that piece of trash does not exist."

Clark walked out of the room to his own desk feeling as if the bottom had dropped out of everything. He was astonished, bewildered, and considerably angered. His great respect for Norman checked his rising indignation and disgust, but with it all was a feeling of growing wonder at the sudden change of motive which had entered the offices of the *Daily News* and would surely threaten to destroy it.

Before noon every reporter, pressman, and employee was informed of the remarkable fact that the paper was going to press without a word about the now infamous movie premiere. The reporters were astonished by the announcement. Everyone in the typesetting and composing rooms had something to say about the unheard of omission. Two or three times during the day when Mr. Norman had occasion to visit the composing rooms, the men stopped their work or glanced around their workstations looking at him curiously. He knew that he was being observed, but said nothing and did not appear to note it.

Their publisher sometimes took the liberty of making minor changes to the paper, but nothing of great importance. He was waiting, deep in thought.

It was not because there were not a great many things in the life of the paper that were contrary to the Spirit of Christ that he did not act at once, but because he was still honestly in doubt concerning what action Jesus would take.

When the *Daily News* was delivered that evening to its subscribers, a note of shock was felt by all who had anticipated the movie story and news of the premiere.

The presence of the review could not have produced anything equal to the effect of its omission. People in the hotels and stores downtown, who had come to Raymond specifically for the premiere, as well as regular subscribers, eagerly opened the paper and searched for mention of the new film; not finding it, they rushed to the newsstands and bought other papers.

A woman bought the paper from a newsstand near the corner of the avenue close to the *News* office, looked over its front page hurriedly, and then angrily confronted the man behind the counter.

"What's the matter with your paper? There's no information at all in here about the premiere. You must have sold me an old paper!"

"Old paper nuthin'!" replied the man indignantly. "That's today's paper. What's the matter with you?"

"But there is no information about the movie premiere here in Raymond. Look for yourself!"

The woman handed the paper to the boy and he glanced at it hurriedly. Then he whistled, while a bewildered look crept over his face. A hasty examination of all his copies of the *News* revealed the remarkable fact that none made so much as a mention of the movie and its opening in Raymond.

"Here, give me another paper!" shouted the customer, "one with information about the premiere. That is after all why I came into town."

She took a copy of a competitor's paper and walked off, while the paper dealer shook his bewildered head. "Something crazy is going on at the *News*. Here, Charley, you mind the shop, I'm going over to the *News* offices to see what's happening."

There were several other paper dealers at the delivery room and they were all angry about the omission.

Mr. Norman was just coming downstairs on his way home, and he paused as he went by the door of the delivery room and looked in.

"What's the matter here, George?" he asked the clerk as he noted the unusual confusion.

"These dealers say they can't sell their copies of the *News* tonight because we didn't carry a story of the movie premiere. There are people coming into town for it. Not a word in the news," replied George, looking curiously at the publisher as so many of the employees had done during the day. Mr. Norman hesitated a moment, then walked into the room and confronted the dealers.

"How many papers do you think you will be unable to sell? Give me a number, and I'll buy them all from you tonight."

"Give them their money, George, and if any of the other dealers come in with the same complaint buy back their copies as well. Is that fair?" he asked the men, who were speechless in response to the unheard-of action on the part of the publisher.

"Fair! Well, I should—But will you keep this up? Will we continue to do this for the benefit of the dealers?"

Mr. Norman smiled slightly but he did not think it was necessary to answer the question.

He walked out of the building and went home. On the way, he could not avoid that constant query, "Would Jesus have done it?" It was not so much with reference to this last transaction as to the entire motive that had urged him on since he made the promise.

The newspaper dealers were unnecessarily suffering because of the action he had taken. Why should they lose money? They were not to blame. He was a rich man and could afford to help them if he chose to do so. He believed, as he went on his way home, that Jesus would have done either what he did or something similar in order to be free from any possible injustice.

He was not deciding these questions for anyone else but himself. He was not in a position to lecture others, and he felt that he could answer only with his own judgment and as to his interpretation of his Master's probable action. He had to some degree anticipated that sales would be affected by his decision, but he was yet to realize the full extent of the loss to the paper if such a policy were continued.

CHAPTER 4

During the week, Ed Norman received numerous letters commenting on the paper's lack of information about the movie premiere scheduled for the previous weekend. A sampling of the reader response was forwarded to his office.

Editor of the *Daily News*:

Dear Sir—I have been thinking for some time of changing my paper. I want a paper that is up-to-date, progressive, and enterprising, supplying what the public demands. The apparent oversight of your paper concerning the review and photos of a European film that will probably be nominated for an Academy Award has convinced me to change to another paper. Please discontinue my subscription.

Very truly yours, _____

The letter had been sent by a Raymond business owner who had been a subscriber for many years.

Publisher of the *Daily News*—Raymond:

Dear Ed—What is this hornet's nest you are stirring in your burg? What is this new policy you have taken up? Hope you don't intend to try to reform the media single-handedly. It's dangerous to experiment much along that line. Take my advice and stick to the enterprising methods that have made your holdings such a success. Give the public what it wants, and let someone else do the dirty work of cleaning up the industry.

Yours, _____

This letter was signed by one of Norman's oldest friends in the newspaper industry.

Ed Norman also received this letter:

My Dear Norman:

I must express my appreciation for what can only be the evidence that you are carrying out your promise no matter what the personal consequences. It is a splendid beginning and no one feels the value of it more than I do. I know something of what it will cost you, but not all. Your pastor,

Henry Maxwell

Mr. Edward Norman received one other letter that morning. He opened it immediately after reading the note from Pastor Maxwell, and it revealed to him something of the loss to his businesses that possibly awaited him.

Mr. Edward Norman,
Publisher of the *Daily News:*

Dear Sir—At the expiration of my advertising limit, you will do me the favor not to continue it as you have done heretofore. I enclose check for payment in full and shall consider my account with your papers closed after date.

Very truly yours, _____

This letter had been sent by one of the largest tobacco dealers in the city, who had been in the habit of inserting a column of conspicuous advertising and paying a very high price for it.

Norman laid this letter down thoughtfully, and then after a moment he took up a copy of his advertising financial spread. There was no obvious connection between the tobacco merchant's withdrawal of advertising and the omission of the movie review, but he could not avoid putting the two together. In fact, he later learned that the tobacco dealer had withdrawn his advertisement because he had heard that the editorial policy of the *Daily News* and its sister Channel 1 TV was about to institute some strange reform policy that would be certain to reduce its subscription list.

The letter did serve to direct Norman's attention to the advertising phase of his paper and his television stations. He had not considered this before.

As he glanced over the profit-loss columns, he could not escape the conviction that Jesus would not allow some of them to advertise in His newspapers or on His stations.

What would He do with the other advertisers of products that kill the body, the soul, and the family? As a member of a church and a respected citizen, he had brought about no special criticism because of the nature of the ads. No one thought anything about it. It was all legitimate business. Why not? He was simply doing what every other businessman in Raymond did. And it was one of the best paying sources of revenue. What would his papers and stations do without this important source of revenue? Could they continue to thrive? He couldn't say, but that was after all not the question he was attempting to answer that week. The question that week was, "What would Jesus do?" Would Jesus advertise alcohol and tobacco products in His newspapers and on His television stations?

Edward Norman pondered the dilemma honestly, and after a prayer for help and wisdom, asked Clark to come into his office.

Clark came in feeling that the paper was in a crisis and prepared for almost anything after his Monday morning experience. This was Thursday.

"Clark," said Norman, speaking slowly and carefully, "I have been looking at our advertising, and I have decided to dispense with some of our contracts as soon as they run out. I would like you to notify our advertising agents and instruct them not to solicit or renew the ads that I have marked here."

He handed the paper to Clark, who took it and seriously examined it.

"This will mean a great loss to the *Daily News* and to Norman Communications. How long do you think you can keep this sort of thing up?" Clark was astounded by his boss's action.

"Clark, if Jesus were the publisher of this newspaper or the manager of a television station, do you think He would permit questionable advertising like this?"

"Well—no—I don't suppose He would. But what does that have to do with us? We can't live like He did. Everyone knows that newspapers and television stations can't survive in today's competitive markets with that kind of policy."

"Why not?" asked Norman quietly.

"Why not? Because they will lose more money than they make!" Clark spoke out with an irritation that he really felt. "We will bankrupt the corporation with this sort of business policy."

"Do you think so?" Norman asked the question not as if he expected an answer, but as if he were talking to himself. After a pause he said:

"Direct Mr. Marks to do as I have said. I believe it is what Christ would do, and as I told you, Clark, that is what I have promised to try to do for a year, regardless of what the results may be. I can't believe there is any way at all that we can justify some of the advertising we are presently carrying.

Clark went back to his desk feeling as if he had been in the presence of a madman. He felt enraged and alarmed, and he could not grasp the meaning of it all. He was sure this policy would ruin Norman Communications and the *Daily News* with it, as soon as it became generally known that the CEO was trying to institute such an impossibly high moral standard. What would become of the business world if this standard were adopted? It would upset every accepted practice and introduce endless confusion. It was simply foolishness. No, it was downright suicide. When Marks was informed of the action, he seconded the managing editor's point of view with some very forceful comments. What was the matter with Norman? Was he insane? Was he going to push this religious fanaticism until it bankrupted the whole corporation?

But Edward Norman had not yet faced his most serious problem. When he arrived in his office Friday morning, he was confronted with the usual program for the Sunday morning edition. The *Daily News* was one of the few evening papers in Raymond to issue a Sunday edition, and it had always been remarkably successful financially. There was an average of one page of literary and religious items to 30 to 40 pages of sports, theater, gossip, fashion, society, and political material. This mixture formed a compelling periodical with great variety, which had always been welcomed by all the subscribers, even the church members, as a Sunday morning necessity.

Edward Norman now faced this fact by asking the question that was beginning to control his life, "What would Jesus do?" If He were a newspaper publisher, would He deliberately plan to place such a collection of reading matter, including the shoddy and cheap, in homes on the one day of the week that ought to be given to something better and holier? He was of course familiar with the regular arguments for the Sunday paper, that the public needed something of this nature, and those especially who did not attend church ought to have something entertaining and instructive to read on Sunday, their only day of rest. But suppose the Sunday morning paper were not profitable? How eager would the publisher then be to supply this need? Edward Norman talked honestly with himself about this.

Taking everything into account, would Jesus publish a Sunday morning paper? It really wasn't a matter of profitability. As a matter of fact, the Sunday *News* paid so well that the corporation would suffer an enormous financial loss if it were discontinued. Besides that, subscribers had already paid for a seven-day paper. Had he any right now to give them less than they supposed they had paid for?

Norman was honestly perplexed by the question. So much was involved in discontinuing the Sunday edition that for the first time, he almost decided to refuse to be guided by the standard of Jesus' probable action. He was sole proprietor of his enterprises, and they were his to shape in any way he wished. And so it was that he determined to call in his top managers and frankly state his motive and purpose. He would begin with the *Daily News*. He sent word for Clark and the other top managers, including the print foreman, the reporters who could be found, and even a few people from the composing room.

"In fact," he told Clark, "gather everyone who happens to be here this early and let's meet down in the mail room." This was a large room, and the men and women came in curiously and perched around on the tables and counters. It was an unusual proceeding, but they all agreed that something peculiar was going on and they were interested in hearing what Mr. Norman had to say.

"I called you in here to let you know about my plans for the *Daily News*. I am instituting certain changes, which I believe to be necessary. I understand that some of the things I have already done may seem strange to you. I just want you to know my motive behind it."

He told his employees what he had already told Clark, and they stared at him incredulously, just as Clark had done.

"Now, in acting on what I believe would be Christ's standard, I have reached a conclusion which will, no doubt, cause even more surprise.

"I have decided that the Sunday edition of the *Daily News* will be discontinued after next Sunday's issue. In that issue, I will state my reasons for discontinuing the service. In order to make up the difference to the subscribers, we will publish a double issue on Saturday, as many evening papers do rather than making an attempt to publish a Sunday edition. I am convinced that from a Christian point of view, more harm than good has been done by our Sunday paper, including the labor that must be expended to get it delivered. I just cannot believe that Jesus would allow it if He were in my place. I'm certain that there will be some difficulty arranging the details of this change with the advertisers and subscribers. I will be responsible for handling that. So far as I can see, any loss will fall directly on me."

Norman looked around the room. No one spoke. He was struck with the realization that in all the years of his career, he had never brought his creative and production staff together in this way. Would Jesus do that? Would He run His newspapers on some loving family plan, where editors, reporters, pressmen, and all meet to discuss and plan a newspaper with God's priorities in mind?

He caught himself drawing back from the facts of unions and office rules and reporters' enterprise and all the cold, business concerns that go into the making of a great newspaper. But still the scene in the mail room would not be forgotten when he returned to his offices and his employees returned to their workstations still with a lack of understanding and unanswered questions about their CEO's remarkable actions.

Clark followed Norman into his office suite for a long, serious talk. He was thoroughly upset, and his protest almost reached the point of resigning his position. Norman guarded himself carefully. Every minute of the one-sided conversation was painful for him, but he felt more than ever the necessity of doing the Christlike thing. Clark was a very valuable man and he would be difficult to replace. Norman determined to hear him out, but in the end, Clark could offer no significant reason for continuing the Sunday paper that answered the question, "What would Jesus do?"

"It comes to this, then," said Clark frankly, "you will bankrupt the paper in 30 days. We might as well face that fact."

"I don't believe that will happen," answered Norman with a strange smile. "I do need to know, however, if you are willing to stand by the *Daily News* whatever the outcome."

"I don't understand you. You are not the same man that I have always known."

"I don't know myself, Clark. Something remarkable has taken hold of me. But I have never been more convinced that my enterprises will succeed if I am willing to do what is right. You have not answered my question. Will you stay with me?"

Clark hesitated a moment before saying yes. Norman shook hands with him and turned to his desk. Clark went back into his office, stirred by a number of conflicting emotions. He had never before known such a stressful but strangely exciting week as this one, and he felt now as if he were connected with an enterprise that might at any moment collapse and ruin him and all those connected with it.

CHAPTER 5

It was another Sunday morning in Raymond, and Reverend Maxwell's sanctuary was crowded once again. Before the service began, Edward Norman attracted great attention. He sat quietly in his usual place about three rows from the pulpit. The Sunday morning issue of the *Daily News,* with the statement of its discontinuance, contained such remarkable language that every reader was genuinely struck by it. Nothing had ever disturbed the business-as-usual mindset of Raymond in this way. The events connected with the *Daily News* were not all the citizens of Raymond were talking about. They were also eagerly discussing the changes that Alexander Powers planned to make at the steel mill, and Milton Wright in his malls and outlet stores. As the service progressed, a distinct wave of excitement filled the pews. Henry Maxwell faced it all with a calmness which indicated the strength and purpose he felt concerning the issues of the past week. His prayers were very helpful, but his sermon was not as easy to describe. What could a pastor possibly preach to his congregation after an entire week of asking, "How would Jesus preach? What might

He say?" It was certain that he could not preach as he had two Sundays before. On Tuesday of the past week, he had stood by the grave of the dead stranger and repeated the familiar words, "Earth to earth, ashes to ashes, dust to dust." His duty served as a reminder to carefully search for the message Jesus would want him to preach the next Sunday.

Now, Sunday had come and the people of First Church were eager to hear what he would tell them. All week long, Maxwell agonized over his sermon preparation, and yet he knew he had not been able to produce a message that properly revealed his ideal of Christ. Nevertheless, no one in First Church could remember ever hearing such a sermon. There was rebuke for sin, especially hypocrisy. Greed was addressed along with the selfish nature of materialism. And yet, shining throughout was a message of love that gathered force as the sermon continued. When it was finished there were those who said in their hearts, *The Spirit moved that sermon.* And they were right.

At the close of the message, Rachel Winslow rose to sing. As always, her singing was greatly appreciated, and yet, something was different.

Rachel was certainly as lovely as ever and her singing as thrilling, but the awareness of her remarkable beauty, which had often detracted from her singing was altogether gone. There was no lack of power in her voice, but there was an added element that shone through of humility and purity which the audience distinctly felt and received.

Before the service closed, Reverend Maxwell asked those who had met the week before to stay again for a few moments of discussion, and any others who were willing to make the pledge could do so at that time. Entering the chapel, he was astonished to see that it was almost filled. This time, a large number of young people had gathered, as well as a few businessmen and officers of the church.

As before, Maxwell asked the group to pray with him. And, as before, there was no doubt in anyone's mind that what they would undertake to do during the week ahead was clearly in line with God's will. They were confident of the presence and direction of the Holy Spirit.

The seekers remained for some time to ask questions and consult together. There was a sense of fellowship that they had never known before in their church membership. Mr. Norman's action was well understood by them all, and he answered several questions.

"How do you expect the discontinuation of the Sunday paper will affect your bottom line?" asked Alexander Powers, who sat next to him.

"I don't know yet. I am certain that we will lose some subscribers and the advertising revenues in question will no doubt be missed."

"Do you have any doubts about your action, Ed? Do you regret it, or worry that it is not what Jesus would do?" asked Reverend Maxwell.

"Not in the least. But for my own satisfaction, let me ask if any of you here think Jesus would publish a Sunday paper for the worldly minded?"

No one spoke for a minute. Then Jasper Chase said, "We seem to agree on that, but I have wondered several times during the week what Jesus would do in certain situations, and I have found that it is not always an easy question to answer."

"I have the same concern," said Virginia Page. She sat by Rachel Winslow. Those who knew Virginia Page wondered how she would succeed in keeping her promise.

"I think perhaps I find it especially difficult to answer that question because I am wealthy. Our

Lord never owned any property, and there is nothing in His example to guide me in the use of mine. I am studying and praying. At times, I think I see clearly what He would do, but the picture is incomplete. For example, what would Jesus do with a few million dollars? I confess that I have not yet come to a conclusion."

"I could tell you what you could do with a part of it," suggested Rachel with a smile.

"That does not trouble me," replied Virginia. "What I am trying to discover is a principle that will enable me to come as close as possible to Christ's actions."

"That will take time," said the minister slowly. Every person in the room was thinking hard about the same thing. Milton Wright shared something of his experience. He was in the process of designing a health and profit-sharing package for his employees, and it was opening up a new world for them. A few of the young men told of their attempts to answer the question of what would Jesus do in some specific situations. To a person, there was agreement that the application of Christian practice in everyday life was a serious thing. It required a knowledge of

Jesus Christ and an insight into His motives that most of them did not yet possess.

After a period of meditation and silent prayer, they adjourned, and went their own ways mulling over their difficulties and their need for divine light.

Rachel Winslow and Virginia Page went out together. Edward Norman and Milton Wright became so interested in their discussion that they walked down the sidewalk past the parsonage and then circled back still in conversation. Jasper Chase and the president of the youth group spoke earnestly in one corner of the room. Alexander Powers and Henry Maxwell remained, even after the others had gone.

"I want you to come down to the mill tomorrow and see the plan I have submitted and talk to the employees. Somehow I feel you could get closer to them than anyone else."

"I don't know about that, but I will come," replied Reverend Maxwell a little sadly. How could he stand before two or three hundred working men and women and give them a message pertinent to their lives? What did he have to say to them that could not be better said from his pulpit? Yet in the moment of weakness, as he asked the question, he rebuked himself for it. What would Jesus do? That was the end of the discussion.

Reverend Maxwell went down the next day and found Powers in his office.

"Come upstairs, and I'll show you what I've been working on," Powers offered.

They went through a machine shop, climbed a long flight of stairs, and entered a large, empty room. It had once been used by the company as a storage facility.

"Since making that promise a week ago I have had a good many things to think about," said Powers, "and among them is this: The mill's board of directors has approved the use of this area, and I plan to have tables assembled and a refreshment center placed in that area over there. My plan is to provide a common area where the employees can come for breaks and to eat lunch. I expect to provide good magazines and Christian reading material." Powers then expressed his desire to bring in an occasional inspirational speaker to address issues about which some employees might have concerns in their everyday lives.

Maxwell looked surprised and asked if the employees would be interested in attending such a gathering.

"Yes, I believe they'll come. These people are among the most intelligent in our city. But most of them are removed from the influence of the church. I asked, 'What would Jesus do?' and besides improving our health insurance program, it seemed to me He would begin to act in some way to add to the lives of these men and women more physical and spiritual comfort. This area and what it represents is a little thing, but I acted in honesty on my first impulse, and I want this to work out. Pastor, I would like you to speak to the employees when they come up for lunch. I've invited them in to see the place, and I want to tell them about the plans I'm working on."

Maxwell was ashamed to admit how uneasy he felt at being asked to speak a few words to a company of workers. How could he speak without notes and thorough preparation to such a crowd? He felt more nervous and apprehensive than he could ever remember. He actually felt afraid to face those men and women, and shrank back simply because they were so different from the Sunday congregation he was familiar with.

There were dozens of folding chairs, benches, and tables in the room, and when the lunch break bell rang, people poured upstairs from the offices and mill below. Seating themselves at the tables, they opened their lunches and began to eat. The refreshment center was a happy surprise with its free coffee and tea. There were also machines for soft drinks and juices. Though most came out of curiosity, all appeared to be pleased with the addition.

The area was large and airy, free from smoke and dust, and warm. At about twenty minutes before one o'clock, Mr. Powers told the assembled group what he had in mind. He spoke very simply, like one who understands thoroughly the character of his audience, and then introduced the Reverend Henry Maxwell of First Church, his pastor, who had consented to speak for a few minutes.

Maxwell never forgot the feeling he had standing before those workers; men and women of diverse races and social classes. Like many other ministers, he had seldom spoken to groups except those comprised of church people, whom he knew well, and were quite a bit like himself. This was a new world to him, and nothing but his new rule of conduct could have made his message easier. He spoke on the subject of satisfaction with life, what caused it, what its real sources were. While he spoke, the First Church minister became aware of how that group of working people were his brothers and sisters in Christ.

It was obvious that the assemblage was pleased. A good many of them shook hands with him before going back to work. Maxwell left the mill feeling good about the words he had spoken. When he reached home, he told his wife how much the experience had meant to him.

That day marked an important shift in his Christian experience, more important than he could have known. It was the beginning of a relationship between him and the world that stretched beyond the walls of his church. It was the first plank laid down to help bridge the chasm between the church and the populace of Raymond.

Alexander Powers returned to his desk that afternoon pleased with the reception his plan had received and the response of his employees to Pastor Maxwell's words. The routine work of his afternoon went easier and faster than he could have imagined. He felt a glow of satisfaction, knowing that he had done as he felt Jesus would do.

It was nearly four o'clock when Powers opened one of the mill's interoffice envelopes, which he supposed contained orders for the purchase of supplies. He ran over the first page of typewritten matter in his usual quick, businesslike manner, before he saw that what he was reading had not been intended for him, but for the supervisor of the transportation department.

He turned over a page mechanically, trying not to read what had not been addressed to him, but before he knew it, he discovered that what he was reading was conclusive evidence that the company was engaged in a systematic violation of the U.S. Interstate Commerce Laws. It was as clear a violation of law as if a private citizen entered a house and robbed the inhabitants. The discrimination shown in rebates was in total contempt of all the statutes. Under the laws of the state it was also a distinct violation of certain provisions recently passed by the legislature. There was no question that what he held in his hands was sufficient evidence to convict the company of willful, intelligent violation of the law.

He dropped the papers onto his desk as if they were poison, and instantly the question flashed across his mind, "What would Jesus do?" He tried to reason with himself by saying it was none of his business. But the papers now before him revealed the entire affair. They had through some carelessness been addressed to him, but that could not be excuse enough to ignore the matter. If he saw a man entering his neighbor's house to steal, would it not be his duty to inform the police? Was a steel mill such a different thing? Was it under a different rule of conduct, so that it could rob the public and defy law and be undisturbed because it was such a powerful organization? What would Jesus do? Then there was his family. Of course, if he took any steps to inform the commission it would mean the loss of his position. His wife and daughter had always enjoyed the good things that money can buy. If he were to come out against this lawlessness, he would be drug through the courts, his motives would be misunderstood, and the whole thing would end in disgrace and the loss of his position. Surely it was none of his business. He could easily get the papers back to the transportation department and no one would be the wiser. Let the illegal actions go on. Let the law be defied. What was it to him? He would work out his plans for bettering the conditions before him now. What more could a man do in an industry where so much was going on anyway that it seemed virtually impossible to live by the Christian standard? But what would Jesus do if He knew the facts? That was the question that confronted Alexander Powers as the day wore into the evening.

The lights in the office had been turned on. The spark-splattered oven and molds for tempering steel continued to operate. Powers sat there as if in a stupor until he heard the whistle blow signaling the shift change.

Powers could hear the familiar click, click of the clocks as the workers filed past the window of the block house just outside. His custom was to leave at six o'clock, the end of the first shift, but tonight was different. He said to his secretary in answer to her quizzical look, "I'm not going just yet. I have something extra to do tonight."

At seven o'clock, anyone who had looked into Powers' office would have seen an unusual sight. He was kneeling beside his desk with his face buried in his hands.

CHAPTER 6

If anyone comes to me and does not hate
his father and mother, his wife and children,
his brothers and sisters—yes, even his
own life—he cannot be my disciple.
And anyone who does not carry his cross
and follow me cannot be my disciple.
Luke 14:26-27

When Rachel Winslow and Virginia Page separated after the meeting at First Church on Sunday, they agreed to continue their conversation the next day. Virginia asked Rachel to come for lunch, and Rachel rang the bell at the Page home about half-past eleven. Virginia herself met her and the two were soon immersed in conversation.

"The fact is," Rachel admitted after they had been talking a few moments, "I cannot reconcile it with what I believe Christ would do. I can't say what someone else would do, but I feel that I should not accept this offer."

"What will you do then?" asked Virginia with great interest.

"I don't know yet. All I know is that I can't do this," she said, indicating the letter on her lap.

Rachel picked up the letter and scanned its contents again. It was from the manager of a touring musical comedy offering her a place with the company. The salary was sizable, as were the future opportunities. The company representative had heard Rachel sing that Sunday morning when the stranger interrupted the service and had been most impressed with her performance. "There's money in that voice and it ought to be used on the stage," his letter stated. The manager wanted a quick reply.

"There's no great virtue in saying 'No' to this offer when I have another one waiting in the wings," Rachel continued. "That's what makes the decision so difficult. But I think I have made up my mind. To tell you the truth, Virginia, I'm completely convinced that Jesus would not want me to use my talent just to make money. But then, there is this concert offer with a reputable company, and I would travel with a manager, a violinist, and a singing ensemble, all talented people. The salary—I mentioned it, didn't I?—is guaranteed to be a staggering amount for the season. But I don't feel satisfied that Jesus would accept that offer, either. What do you think, Virginia?"

"You mustn't ask me to decide for you," Virginia replied with a slight smile. "I believe Reverend Maxwell was right when he said we must each decide according to the standard we set for ourselves to walk in His steps. I am having a difficult time myself deciding what He would do."

"Are you really?" Rachel asked. She rose and walked over to the window and looked out. Virginia came and stood by her. The two women were silent for a moment and then suddenly Virginia spoke passionately.

"Rachel, what does all this mean to you in light of our question, 'What would Jesus do?' It's frustrating to think that the world in which I was brought up continues year after year to be preoccupied with fashion and food and cars, spending its money on lavish homes and luxuries. Occasionally, to ease our consciences, we may donate a little something to charity. It's hardly a grave personal sacrifice. I was educated in one of the most prestigious schools in the country and launched into society with nearly unlimited resources. I have an enviable life. I can travel or stay at home. Realistically, I can do as I please, gratifying almost any want or desire. And yet, when I honestly try to imagine Jesus living the life I have lived and am expected to live, I condemn myself for being one of the most uncaring, selfish, useless creatures in all the world. It has been weeks since I could think about the world outside this window, without a feeling of revulsion toward myself."

Virginia turned away and paced the length of the room. Rachel watched her while trying desperately to repress the specter of her own growing definition of discipleship. As a Christian, of what use was her own singing talent? Was the sale of her talent for impressive money, a concert tour, beautiful clothes, the enjoyment of applause and adulation worth turning her back on this eternal question, "What would Jesus do?"

She was full of energy, in good health, and had been blessed with an impressive and powerful singing voice. She knew what her talent could provide. The words Virginia spoke struck her with force. Despite their differences, there were a great many similarities between the two friends.

When lunch was announced, the women were joined by Virginia's grandmother, Mrs. Page, a beautiful, mature woman, and Virginia's brother Rollin, a young man of questionable ambition, except when it came to Rachel Winslow. When she visited, Rollin always planned to be at home.

These three were all that remained of the Page family. Virginia's mother had died ten years before. Her father, who had made his fortune in banking, had been gone less than a year. Grandmother Page, a southern woman in birth and training, had all the traditions and attitudes that accompany wealth and social standing. She was a shrewd, careful businesswoman. The family property and wealth were invested, in large measure, under her personal care. Virginia's portion, however, was without restriction. She had been trained by her father to understand the ways of the business world, and even her fastidious grandmother had been compelled to acknowledge her ability to take care of her own money.

Perhaps two persons could not be found anywhere less capable of understanding a woman like Virginia than Mrs. Page and Rollin. Rachel, who had known the family since childhood, could not help thinking about the obstacles Virginia would have to overcome right there in her home once she decided how Jesus would have her follow in His steps. During lunch, Rachel pondered Virginia's confession in the living room, and with regret, pictured the scene that would inevitably occur between Mrs. Page and her granddaughter.

"I understand that you intend to perform professionally, Rachel," Mrs. Page commented.

"You'll be a delight," Rollin interjected.

Rachel felt her cheeks glow with embarrassment and annoyance. "Who told you?" she asked. Virginia, who had been silent and reserved, suddenly appeared ready to join in.

"Oh, we hear a thing or two on the street. Besides, everyone saw the tour representative at church two weeks ago. He doesn't go to church to hear the preaching, you know. In fact, I know someone else who doesn't go for the preaching, not when there's something better to hear."

Rachel answered quietly, "You're mistaken, Rollin. I'm not going on tour."

"That's a pity. You'd be a hit. Everyone says so."

This time Rachel flushed with genuine anger. Before she could say anything, Virginia broke in:

"Whom do you mean by 'everyone'?"

"Whom do you think? I mean all the people who have heard Rachel sing. That would pretty much be the people at First Church. Where else would they hear her? It's a shame that the public has no other opportunity to enjoy her talent."

"Let's talk about something else," said Rachel sharply. Mrs. Page glanced at her and spoke with a gentle courtesy.

"My dear, Rollin never could be subtle. He's like his father in that way. However, we are all curious to know something of your plans. Old friends should know what's going on with you. Virginia has already told us of your concert tour offer."

"I supposed of course that was public knowledge," said Virginia, smiling across the table.

"Of course," replied Rachel hastily. "I understand your interest, Mrs. Page. Actually, Virginia and I have been talking about my future. I have decided not to accept the offer, and that is as far as I have gone at present."

Rachel was conscious of the fact that the conversation had, up to this point, been narrowing her options to one that would absolutely satisfy her own judgment of Jesus' probable action. Somehow what Rollin Page had said and his manner of saying it, hastened her decision.

"Rachel, would you mind telling us your reasons for refusing the offer? It seems to me to be a great opportunity for a young woman. Don't you think the public should have the chance to hear you sing? I feel the same as Rollin does about that. A voice like yours belongs to a grander audience than Raymond and First Church."

Rachel Winslow was a woman of great reserve. She shrank from making her plans or her thoughts public. But with all her resolve, she gave a thoroughly frank, truthful expression of her most personal feelings. She spoke to Mrs. Page in one of those rare moments of candor that added to the attractiveness of her character.

"I have no other reason than a conviction that Jesus Christ would do the same thing," she said, looking into Mrs. Page's eyes with a clear, earnest gaze.

Mrs. Page flushed and Rollin stared in amazement. Before her grandmother could say anything, Virginia spoke.

"Grandmother, you know we promised to make that our standard of conduct for a year. Reverend Maxwell's challenge was simple to all who heard it—ask yourselves the question, 'What would Jesus do?' in this or any situation. We have not arrived at our decisions in haste. The difficulty in knowing what Jesus would do has perplexed Rachel and me a great deal."

Mrs. Page looked sharply at Virginia before she said anything.

"Of course I understand Reverend Maxwell's statement, but it is very difficult to put that philosophy into practice. At the time, I felt confident that those who made such a promise would discover what a difficult proposition it is and abandon it as idealistic and absurd. I have nothing to say about Rachel's affairs, but," she paused and continued with a sharpness that was new to Rachel, "I hope you have not taken on any foolish notions of this kind, Virginia."

"I have a great many notions," replied Virginia quietly. "Whether they are foolish or not depends upon my right understanding of what Jesus would do. As soon as I find out I will do it."

"Excuse me, ladies," said Rollin, rising from the table. "This conversation is getting a little deep for me."

He left the dining room and there was silence for a moment. Mrs. Page was angry with Rachel.

"I am older by many years than you two young ladies," she said. "I don't wish to burst your bubble, but I must say that what you have promised in a moment of great emotion is for all intents and purposes impossible to fulfill."

"What are you saying, grandmother? Are you telling us that we cannot possibly act as our Lord Jesus would? Or do you mean that, if we try, we will offend the customs and prejudices of proper society?" asked Virginia.

"It is not required! It is not necessary! Besides how can you act with any—" Mrs. Page paused, broke off her sentence, and then turned to Rachel. "What will your mother have to say about your decision? For heaven's sake, what do you expect to do with your voice anyway?"

"I don't yet know what Mother will say," Rachel answered, shying away from trying to predict her mother's probable answer. If there were a woman in all Raymond with great ambitions for her daughter's success as a singer, Mrs. Winslow was that woman.

"Oh, my dear, I believe you will see it in a different light when you have had time to think it through," continued Mrs. Page rising from the table. "An opportunity like this doesn't come along every day. I know you will come to regret your decision."

Rachel's response contained a hint of the struggle she was experiencing, and after a bit she excused herself, with a thank-you for the luncheon. Virginia saw her to the door, but not a word was exchanged between them. Waiting for a taxi, she analyzed the last two hours and the disturbing feeling that her departure would be followed by a painful conversation between Virginia and her grandmother. As she would later learn, Virginia's conversation with her grandmother did bring her much closer to an understanding of her place in the world and how she was to put her money to use.

CHAPTER 7

Rachel was glad to escape and be by herself. A plan was slowly forming in her mind, and she wanted to be alone to carefully think it through. But before she could reach her taxi, she was annoyed to find Rollin Page walking toward her.

"Sorry to disturb your thoughts, Rachel, but I happened to be going your way and thought I might be able to give you a lift. The truth is, I followed you out of the house."

"I didn't see you," said Rachel briefly.

"I wouldn't mind that if I knew you thought of me once in a while," said Rollin. Taking her arm, he steered her over to an impressive foreign sports car parked at the curb.

Rachel was surprised, but not startled. She had known Rollin as a boy, and there was a time when they had each felt comfortable in the other's presence. Lately, however, something in Rachel's manner had put an end to that. She was used to his direct attempts at compliments and was sometimes amused and often annoyed by them. Today, she honestly wished him to be anywhere else.

"Do you ever think of me, Rachel?" asked Rollin opening the door for her.

"Quite often!" said Rachel with a smile.

"Are you thinking of me now?"

"Yes. That is—yes—I am."

"What are you thinking?"

"Do you want me to be absolutely truthful?"

"Of course."

"Then I was wishing that I wasn't in this car with you."

Rollin bit his lip and looked uncomfortable.

"Now Rachel, you know how I feel. What makes you treat me like you do? You used to like me a little, you know."

"Did I? Of course we used to get on very well when we were kids, but we're older now," Rachel said, trying to keep her voice light and carefree.

They drove along in silence. Traffic was heavy and there were streams of people along the sidewalks. Stopping at a light, Rachel glanced over and saw Jasper Chase in his car next to them. He saw Rachel and Rollin and nodded. Rollin watched Rachel closely.

"I wish I were Jasper Chase. Then perhaps I would stand some chance with you," he said moodily.

Rachel blushed in spite of herself. She decided not to respond and moved closer to the door. Rollin seemed determined to speak his mind, and Rachel seemed helpless to prevent him.

"You know how I feel about you, Rachel. Isn't there any hope for us? I know I could make you happy. I've loved you for so many years—"

"Well, how old do you think I am?" broke in Rachel with a nervous laugh. His blatant disclosure had shaken her out of her usual poise.

"You know what I mean," Rollin continued doggedly. "And you have no right to laugh at me just because I'm truthful about my feelings for you."

"I'm not laughing at you," Rachel said after a short hesitation. "It's just that it's useless for you to talk like this."

"Would—that is—do you think—if you gave me time I would—"

"No!" said Rachel. She spoke firmly; perhaps, she thought afterward, she had spoken harshly.

They continued to drive in silence, and Rachel was relieved to see that they were near her home. She was anxious for this uncomfortable scene to end.

Turning off the avenue onto one of the quieter streets, Rollin spoke suddenly and forcefully. There was almost a note of dignity in his voice that was new to Rachel.

"Rachel, I love you and I want to marry you. Is there any hope you will ever consent?"

"None," Rachel spoke decidedly.

"Will you tell me why?" He asked the question as if he had a right to a truthful answer.

"Because I don't feel toward you as a woman ought to feel toward the man she marries."

"In other words, you don't love me?"

"No—I don't and I can't."

"Why?" That was another question, and Rachel was a little surprised that he would ask.

"Because—," she hesitated for fear she might say too much in an attempt to speak the exact truth.

"Just tell me why. You can't hurt me more than you have already."

"Well, I do not and I cannot love you because you have no purpose in life. What do you ever do to make the world better? You spend your time thinking up new ways to amuse yourself. There is nothing in that kind of life that would attract me."

"I see," said Rollin with a bitter laugh.

He suddenly stopped in front of her house and jumped out to open her door. As she stepped out, he bowed gravely, returned to the car, and drove away. Rachel went into the house and hurried up to her room.

When she had time to replay the events of the afternoon, she found herself condemned by the very judgment she had passed on Rollin Page. What purpose did she have in life? She had studied music with one of the best teachers in Europe. Then she returned to Raymond and took her place in the First Church choir. She had been home almost a year now and up until two Sundays ago, she had been quite satisfied with herself and her position. She had shared her mother's ambition and anticipated her share of triumphs in the music world. What possible purpose could her life have other than the ordinary career as a singer?

How could she make her life count for something—make a difference in the world? What would Jesus do? She could earn a fortune with her voice. She knew that, not necessarily as a matter of personal pride or professional ego, but simply as a fact. A fact she had been happy to acknowledge until two weeks ago. Until then, she had fully intended to use her voice totally for her own glory and reward. Was that much different, after all, than what Rollin Page lived for?

Rachel sat in her room a long time and finally went downstairs, resolved to have a frank talk with her mother about the concert tour offer and the new plan which was gradually shaping in her mind. She had already had one talk with her mother and knew that she fully expected her to accept the offer and get her career underway.

"Mother," Rachel said, coming directly to the point, "I have decided not to go on tour with the company. Before you say anything, I hope you will hear me out. I have a good reason."

Mrs. Winslow was fond of good company, ambitious for distinction in society and devoted, according to her own definition of success, to the success of her children. Her youngest, Louis, two years younger than Rachel, was ready to graduate from a military academy in the summer. Meanwhile, she and Rachel were at home together. Rachel's father, like Virginia's, had died a few years earlier, and both women found themselves chafing under the restraints of their present circumstances. In fact, at this point in her life, Rachel found herself completely antagonistic toward her mother. Mrs. Winslow waited for Rachel to continue.

"You know the promise I made two weeks ago, Mother?"

"Reverend Maxwell's promise?"

"No, mine. You know what it was, Mother?"

"I suppose I do. Of course all Christians mean to imitate Christ and follow Him, as far as that can be done in this day and age. But what has that to do with the concert tour?"

"It has everything to do with it. After asking, 'What would Jesus do?' and going to the Bible for wisdom, I have been obliged to say that I don't believe Jesus would want me to use my voice in that way."

"Why? Is there something wrong with such a career?"

"No, I don't suppose so."

"Do you presume to sit in judgment of other people who pursue singing careers? Are you saying they are doing something that Christ would not do?"

"Mother, I want you to understand. I'm not judging anyone. I simply want to choose my own course. I just feel a strong conviction that Jesus would do something else."

"What else?" Mrs. Winslow had not yet lost her temper. She did not understand the situation nor did she understand Rachel, but she was determined that her daughter's course should be as distinguished as her natural gifts promised. And she felt confident that when the religious excitement at First Church died down, Rachel would go on pursuing her public career according to the wishes of her family. She was totally unprepared for Rachel's next remark.

"What else might I do? I'll tell you what else, Mother. I want to give myself to something that has lasting meaning—something that will help others. Mother, I have made up my mind to use my voice in some way that's better than pleasing fashionable audiences, making money, or even gratifying my own love of singing. I want to do something that will satisfy me when I ask: 'What would Jesus do?' I am not satisfied when I think of myself as a performer."

Rachel spoke with a vigor and earnestness that surprised her mother. Consequently, Mrs.

Winslow was angry; and on such occasions, she rarely tried to conceal her feelings.

"This is absurd! Rachel, you are talking like a fanatic! What can you do?"

"The world has been served wonderfully by men and women who have used their gifts for something other than money and prestige. Why shouldn't I do the same thing? Why should I feel compelled to place a market value on my talent? After all, it is a gift. You know, Mother, you think of my career in terms of financial and worldly success. But, since I made my promise two weeks ago, I have been unable to imagine Jesus going on a concert tour if for no other reason than the lifestyle that is expected in that world."

Mrs. Winslow rose and then sat down again. With great effort, she composed herself.

"What do you intend to do then? You haven't answered my question."

"For the time being, I will continue to sing in the church, Rachel responded. I have committed myself to do so through the spring. During the week, I plan to sing at the meetings sponsored by the City Union Mission downtown."

"What! Rachel, that is just crazy! You have no idea what you are saying? Do you know what sort of people you will encounter in that part of the city? You may as well throw your talent in the gutter!"

Rachel almost shook in the face of her mother's outburst. For a moment, she shrank back and was silent. Then she spoke firmly:

"I know very well what I will encounter. That's the reason I'm going. Reverend and Mrs. Gray have been working there for weeks. I learned only this morning that they are asking singers from the churches to help. The meetings are being held in a storefront in a part of the city where Christians are desperately needed. And I fully intend to help all I can, Mother!"

Rachel cried out with the first passionate utterance she had yet used, "I want to do something that makes a difference. I know you don't understand, but I can't help asking what I have ever done to eliminate some of the suffering around me? How much have I denied myself or given out of a sense of personal sacrifice to better the city in which I live? How often have I imitated the life of Jesus in the world around me? Must I go on doing as the world selfishly dictates and never know the pain that my selfishness causes?"

"Are you preaching to me?" asked Mrs. Winslow slowly. Understanding her mother's words, Rachel rose to her feet.

"No. I am preaching to myself," she replied gently. She paused a moment as if she thought her mother would say something more. Then she resigned herself to the silence and returned to her room. She was certain that she could expect no sympathy or understanding from her mother.

She knelt near a chair. In the two weeks since Henry Maxwell's church had faced that shabby-looking figure with the faded cap, more members of his congregation had been driven to their knees than during the entire previous term of his pastorate.

When Rachel rose, her face was wet with tears. She sat thoughtfully on her bed for a little while, and then picked up the phone and dialed Virginia's number. After a brief conversation, she went downstairs and told her mother that she and Virginia were going down to the evangelistic meeting that evening.

"Don't worry," Rachel whispered. "Virginia's uncle, Dr. West, will go with us. He's a friend of the Grays and attended some of their meetings last winter."

Mrs. Winslow said nothing. Her manner clearly indicated her complete disapproval of Rachel's course, and Rachel felt her unspoken bitterness.

About seven o'clock, the doctor and Virginia appeared, and together, the three left for the meeting located in the Rectangle, the most dangerous district in Raymond. In addition to Raymond's tenement district, the Rectangle included a barren field used in the summer by carnivals. It was shut in by rows of bars and clubs. The city leaders turned a blind eye to the prostitutes and drug dealers who openly worked the corners.

Raymond's First Church had never made any effort to help solve the problems inherent in this seamy area. It was too dirty, coarse, and unseemly for any kind of concerned involvement. There had once been an attempt by various churches to clean up the area by occasionally sending singers, children's workers, or sidewalk preachers to hand out tracts. But throughout the years, the First Church of Raymond had ignored any attempt to make the Rectangle district any less a stronghold of despair and hopelessness.

However, a brave evangelist and his wife had moved into an abandoned storefront and begun to hold meetings in this heart of "Sodom." It was the spring of the year, and the evenings were beginning to be pleasant. The evangelist had asked for the help of area Christians, and he had received more than the usual amount of encouragement. But he and his wife were feeling the need for volunteers to replace those, once enthusiastic, who now had begun to participate less and less, especially those with musical ability. To add to the shortage of qualified musicians, the keyboard player had become ill during the meetings on the Sunday just past.

"The meeting will be small tonight, John," said his wife, as they walked into the storefront chapel a little after seven o'clock to begin sweeping and arranging chairs.

"I'm afraid you're right," Reverend Gray answered. He was a small, energetic man, with a pleasant voice and the courage of a prize fighter. He had already made friends in the neighborhood, and one of his converts had just come in to help get the room in order.

It was after eight o'clock when Alexander Powers closed the door of his office and started for home. He was parked a half block from the corner of the Rectangle district. He was used to the neighborhood and had parked at the same stretch of curb for the last 15 years. Approaching his well-shined black automobile, he was surprised to hear a familiar voice coming from a nearby building.

He was certain it was the voice of Rachel Winslow.

What was she singing? And how did Rachel Winslow happen to be performing in this God-forsaken part of the city? Several windows nearby went up. Some men quarreling outside a bar stopped and listened. Other people were walking rapidly in the direction of the storefront chapel. Surely, he thought, Rachel's voice had never sounded sweeter. What was it she was singing? Alexander Powers paused and listened.

Where He leads me I will follow,
Where He leads me I will follow,
Where He leads me I will follow,
I'll go with Him, with Him
All the way!

The brutal and coarse life of the Rectangle district seemed to stop in its tracks for a few minutes as the song, as pure as the surroundings were vile, floated out from the storefront and into the buildings nearby.

The steel superintendent turned briefly toward the lighted storefront. Then he stopped. After a moment of indecision, he opened his car door, crawled in, and started home. But before he reached the corner, he knew he had settled for himself the question of what Jesus would do.

CHAPTER 8

If anyone would come after me,
he must deny himself and take up
his cross and follow me.
Matthew 16:24

Henry Maxwell paced back and forth in his study. It was Wednesday, and he had started to think through the sermon for his midweek service. Through his study window, he could see the tall chimney of the steel mill. The roofs of the block of storefronts where Reverend Gray was holding meetings in his storefront chapel peered only slightly above the other buildings of the Rectangle district. Every time he passed the window, Reverend Maxwell turned to look. After a while he sat down and placed a large piece of paper on the desk in front of him. He paused for a few thoughtful moments and then began to write in large letters at the top of the page:

WHAT THINGS WOULD JESUS
DO IN THIS PASTORATE?

1. Jesus would live in a simple, plain manner, without needless luxury on the one hand or undue austerity on the other.

2. Jesus would preach fearlessly, without regard for the social status or the wealth of those in attendance.

3. Jesus would find a practical way to show His sympathy and love for the common people as well as for the well-to-do, educated, and refined people who make up the First Church congregation.

4. Jesus would identify with the great causes of humanity in some personal way that would call for self-denial and suffering.

5. Jesus would preach against addictive vices that enslave, such as drugs, alcohol, and pornography.

6. Jesus would make friends with those who dwell in the vilest parts of the city.

7. Jesus would give up the summer trip to Europe this year. (I have been abroad twice and cannot claim any special need of rest. I am well, and could forego this pleasure, using the money for someone who needs a vacation more than I. No doubt, there are plenty of people in the city who would qualify.)

Maxwell was conscious that his list of Jesus' probable actions was painfully lacking in intellectual depth and power, but he was simply looking for specific suggestions of how Jesus' conduct might influence change in the city of Raymond. Nearly every point he put down on the paper meant, for him, a complete reversal of principles that had dictated his ministry for years. Yet he still searched deeper for sources of the Christlike spirit. He did not attempt to write any more, but sat at his desk absorbed in his effort to catch more of the spirit of Jesus in his own life.

He was so absorbed by his searching that he did not hear the doorbell ring. Soon he was roused by his wife who announced that a caller was waiting downstairs. She handed him a card, and he was pleased to see that it was Reverend Gray.

Maxwell stepped to the head of the stairs and asked Gray to come up to his office. Gray came right up and quickly stated the reason for his call.

"I need your help, Reverend Maxwell. I'm sure you've heard that we have had wonderful meetings down in the Rectangle district for the past two nights. One of your members, Rachel Winslow, has done more with her voice than I could ever do with my preaching. Our building can no longer contain the crowds.

"Yes. I've heard. It's the first time people in that part of town have been able to hear her sing. I'm not surprised they are coming."

"It's been a real eye-opener for my wife and me, and a great encouragement in our work. But I have a favor to ask; would it be possible for you to come down and preach tonight? I am suffering from a heavy cold and I don't quite trust my voice. I know it's asking a lot of a busy man like yourself, so if you can't make it, just tell me and I will try to find someone else."

"I'm sorry, but tonight is our regular midweek service," began Henry Maxwell. Then he saw the preacher's disappointment and added, "But, I should be able to arrange something. Count me in."

Gray thanked him and rose to go.

"Why don't you stay a minute, Reverend Gray. Perhaps we could have a word of prayer together?"

"I'd like that," said Gray simply.

The two men knelt together in the study. Henry Maxwell prayed like a child, and Gray wiped away his tears. There was something moving about the way Maxwell, who had lived his ministerial life within such narrow boundaries, now begged for the wisdom and strength to deliver a meaningful message to the people from the Rectangle district.

When they finished, Gray rose and held out his hand. "God bless you, Reverend Maxwell. I'm sure the Spirit will give you a powerful message tonight."

Henry Maxwell made no answer. He did not even trust himself to say that he hoped so. But he thought of his promise and it brought him a certain peace that was refreshing to his heart and mind alike.

When the First Church congregation assembled in the chapel that evening, an unusually large number of people were present. Since that remarkable Sunday morning, attendance at the midweek service had soared to heights unequaled in the history of First Church. Reverend Maxwell wasted no time getting to the point.

"I have been asked to preach down in the Rectangle district tonight, and I feel this is what Jesus would want me to do. I will let you decide whether you want to continue with this meeting tonight. I personally believe that the best plan would be for some of you to go down to the Rectangle district with me and be prepared to counsel and pray with those we hope will be committing their lives to the Lord. The rest of you should remain here and pray that the Spirit will go with us."

In response, half a dozen men and women volunteered to go with the pastor, and the rest stayed behind in the chapel to pray. Maxwell realized as he left the room that probably in his entire congregation there were fewer than a handful of individuals capable of successfully leading others in a prayer of salvation.

When Maxwell and his company of volunteers reached the Rectangle district, the storefront was already crowded. So crowded in fact that they had difficulty getting to the platform. Rachel was there with Virginia and Jasper Chase who had escorted them tonight in place of Dr. West.

The meeting began with a solo by Rachel, who then asked the people to join with her on the chorus. By the time she was finished, every available foot of standing room had been taken. The night was mild and the doors were wide open providing a view from the street. Following the singing and a prayer by one of the city pastors, Gray stated the reason for his inability to preach and introduced "Brother Maxwell of First Church."

"Who's that?" asked a hoarse voice from the back.

"He's the preacher at the First Church. We've got a bunch of the upper crust here tonight."

"Did you say First Church? I know that guy. My landlord owns the front pew up there," someone added. A trickle of laughter began in the back as people realized the speaker was a bartender.

"Throw out the lifeline. Throw out the lifeline, someone's stinkin' . . . ," hammed a drunk standing just inside the open doors. His improvisation brought more laughter and jeers from the back. As those in the front turned in the direction of the disturbance, someone called out, "We don't need your kind around here." And then another voice said, "Hey, let's give them a chance. How about another song?"

Henry Maxwell stood up, and a great wave of terror swept through him. This was not like preaching to the well-dressed, respectable, good-mannered people up on the boulevard. He began to speak, but the confusion increased. Gray went down into the crowd, but that did not seem to quiet the disturbance. Reverend Maxwell raised his arm and his voice. The crowd inside began to pay some attention, but the noise on the outside increased. In a few minutes, the audience was beyond his control. He turned to Rachel with a sad smile.

"Sing something, Rachel. I believe they will listen to you," he said, and then sat down and covered his face with his hands.

Rachel felt fully equal to this opportunity. With Virginia at the piano, she began to sing.

Savior, I follow on,
Guided by Thee,
Seeing not yet the hand
That leadeth me.
Hushed be my heart and still
Fear I no farther ill,
Only to meet Thy will,
My will shall be.

Rachel had not finished the first line before the people in the chapel and on the sidewalk outside turned to listen, hushed and reverent. By the end of the first verse, the crowd was subdued and listening intently. Of what importance were the flippant, perfumed, critical audiences in concert halls compared with this dirty, drunken mass of humanity, trembling, weeping, and growing sadly thoughtful under the spell of this young woman and her extraordinary voice. Reverend Maxwell raised his head and saw the transformed crowd. In that vision, he caught a glimpse of what Rachel had been so determined to discover. That is, how would Jesus want to use such a voice?

Jasper Chase sat with his eyes on Rachel, and his greatest longing as an ambitious author was swallowed up in his thought of what Rachel Winslow's love might mean to him. And hidden in the shadows outside the building stood the last person anyone might have expected to see at a service such as this—Rollin Page, who, jostled on every side by the type of people he rarely came in contact with, seemed indifferent to his surroundings and at the same time, mesmerized by the power of Rachel's singing. Intrigued, he had slipped over for a quick look. Neither Rachel nor Virginia saw him that night.

When Rachel's song was finished, Maxwell rose again. This time he felt calmer. *What would Jesus do in this circumstance,* he asked himself? Inspired by the question, he spoke as he had never spoken before. He looked out at the people standing and sitting in front of him and was overwhelmed with caring for their pain. What was Christianity? A calling of sinners, not the righteous, to repentance. How would Jesus speak?

What would He say? He could not yet know all that His message would include, but he felt sure of a part of it. And from that certainty, he spoke. Never before had he felt such compassion for the multitude. During his ten years at First Church, the "multitude" had been nothing more than a vague, dangerous, dirty, troublesome element in society. They were the masses who inhabited the world, outside the church building and outside his reach, an admission that caused him an unpleasant twinge of conscience.

But tonight, he asked himself whether, after all, this was not just about the kind of "multitude" Jesus faced most often. This thought gave him a rush of genuine emotion—of love for these people. He thought that this must be one of the best indications a preacher ever has that he is living close to the heart of the world. It is easy to love an individual sinner, especially if he is personally interesting. To love a multitude of sinners is distinctively a Christlike quality.

When the meeting closed, no special interest was shown. No one stayed to pray or be counseled. The crowd rapidly melted away from the improvised chapel and headed back to the bars. As if making up for lost time, the commerce of the Rectangle district began to move again in earnest. Maxwell and his little party, including Virginia, Rachel, and Jasper Chase, walked down past the row of bars until they reached the corner where their cars were parked.

"This is a terrible area," Maxwell commented. "I never gave these people much thought before tonight. It doesn't seem possible that Christians would have any influence here."

"Do you think anyone can ever clean up this eyesore?" asked Jasper Chase.

"I've been giving a lot of thought lately about what Christians might do to remove the curse of drugs, gambling, alcohol, and prostitution. What if we all acted together against it? What if the pastors and church members of Raymond moved as a united front? What would Jesus do? Would He keep silent? Would He vote to license and protect these purveyors of crime and death?"

He was talking to himself more than to the others. He remembered that he had always been silent in the pulpit about these damning vices. Few of the church members ever raised a voice or seemed concerned about the suffering that existed just a few city blocks away. "What would Jesus do?" Could he answer that question? Would the

Master preach against these evils and the people who promote them if He lived today? How would Jesus preach and act? Suppose Christians thought nothing could really be done and at least, the revenues from these vices could be put to good use. Or suppose the church members themselves owned these questionable establishments or the property where they stood—what then? He knew that those were the facts in Raymond. What would Jesus do?

Reverend Maxwell climbed the stairs to his study the next morning with that question still only partly answered. He had thought about it all night and into the next morning. He was still considering it and seemed to be reaching some conclusions when the *Daily News* was tossed on the porch. His wife brought it up and sat down a few minutes while he read to her.

The *Daily News* was at present the most sensational paper in Raymond. That is, it was being edited in such a remarkable fashion that its subscribers had never been so excited over a newspaper before. First, they had noticed the absence of questionable entertainment news, and gradually it began to dawn on them that the newspaper no longer printed detailed descriptions

of crime or scandals in private life. Then they
noticed that alcohol and tobacco advertisements
had been dropped, along with a few others of a
questionable nature. The discontinuance of the
Sunday edition caused the greatest comment of all,
and now the editorials were creating a stir. A quote
from the Monday paper demonstrated that
Edward Norman was keeping his promise. The
editorial was headed:

THE MORAL SIDE OF POLITICAL QUESTIONS

The editor of the *News* has always
advocated the principles of the political party
at present in power, and has heretofore
discussed all political questions from the
standpoint of expediency, or of belief in the
party as opposed to other political
organizations. Hereafter, to be perfectly honest
with all our readers, the editor will present and
discuss all political questions from the
standpoint of right and wrong. In other words,
the first question asked in this office about any
political question will not be, "Is it in the best
interest of a political party?" or, "Is it in
keeping with the principles laid down in a
particular party's political platform?" No, the
first question asked will be, "Is this measure in

accordance with the spirit and teachings of Jesus as the author of the highest standard of living known to men?" That is, the moral side of every political question will be considered its most important side, and the position taken by this newspaper publisher will be that nations as well as individuals are under the same law to do all things to the glory of God as their first rule.

The same principle will be observed in this office toward candidates for offices of responsibility. Regardless of party politics, the publisher of the *Daily News* will do everything possible to promote the best men for positions of power and will not knowingly support any candidate who does not measure up, no matter how much he may be endorsed by the party. The first question asked about the man or woman and his or her right to hold office will be, "Is this the right candidate for this office?" "Does this candidate have the skills necessary to carry out the responsibilities of the office?" "Is the candidate right for the position?"

The citizens of Raymond read the editorial and rubbed their eyes in amazement. A good many of them with strong party affiliations responded promptly by writing letters asking that their subscriptions be canceled. The paper continued to come out, however, and was eagerly read by thousands all over the city. However, by the end of a week, Edward Norman knew well enough that he was quickly losing a large number of subscribers. Nevertheless, he faced the fact calmly, and tried to assure Clark, the managing editor, who was grimly anticipating ultimate bankruptcy; especially since Monday's editorial.

Tonight, as Maxwell read to his wife, he could see in almost every column the evidence of Norman's conscientious obedience to his promise. There was an absence of slangy, sensational headlines. The reading matter under the headlines was also in keeping with the strictest standards of tasteful journalism. He noticed in two columns that the reporters identified themselves with a byline and there was now a distinct style and dignity in their contributions.

"So Norman is encouraging his reporters and editorial writers to identify themselves. He talked with me about that. It is a good thing. It fixes the responsibility for certain items where it belongs and raises the standard of the work. A good thing all around for both the public and the writers."

Maxwell suddenly paused. His wife looked up from some work she was doing, and noticed that he was reading something with the utmost interest. "Listen to this, Mary," he said, after a moment of mild shock.

"This morning Alexander Powers, superintendent of production at Raymond Steel Mill submitted his resignation, citing the fact that certain information had fallen into his hands; information that indicated that the company had knowingly violated the Interstate Commerce Law and certain state laws. Mr. Powers stated in his resignation that he could no longer withhold the information he possesses. He stated that he had placed the evidence in question into the hands of the Commission so that the appropriate action could be taken.

"This newspaper wishes to comment on this action by Mr. Powers. In the first place, he has nothing to gain by this action. In addition, he has voluntarily given up a valuable position, when, by keeping silent he might have retained it. In the second place, we believe his action ought to receive the approval of all thoughtful, honest citizens who believe in seeing the law obeyed and lawbreakers brought to justice. In a case like this, where evidence against a major industry is generally understood to be almost impossible to obtain, it is the general belief that the officers of the company are often in possession of incriminating facts but do not consider it to be their responsibility to inform the authorities. The entire result of this evasion of responsibility on the part of those who are responsible is demoralizing to every person connected with the company. The publisher of this newspaper recalls the statement made by a prominent CEO in this city a few months ago that nearly every employee in a certain department of the company understood that large sums of money were made by shrewd violations of the law. These knowledgeable individuals admired the shrewdness with which the crime was committed, and declared that they would all do the same if they were in a position to attempt it.[1]

"It is not necessary to say that such an unprincipled view of business is destructive to all the nobler and higher standards of conduct, and

---

[1] This was actually said in one of the General Offices of a great Western railroad, to the author's knowledge.

no person can live in such an atmosphere of unpunished dishonesty and lawlessness without experiencing the tragedy of wrecked character.

"In our judgment, Mr. Powers did the only thing an honest person could do. He has rendered brave and useful service to the state and the general public. It is not always an easy matter to determine the relations that exist between the individual citizen and his fixed duty to the public. In this case, there is no doubt in our minds that the step which Mr. Powers has taken commends itself to every person who believes in law and its enforcement. There are times when the individual must act for the people in ways that will mean sacrifice and loss. Mr. Powers will be misunderstood and misrepresented, but there is no question that his course will be approved by every citizen who wishes to see the powerful corporations as well as the weakest individual stand accountable to the same standard. Mr. Powers has done all that a loyal, patriotic citizen could do. It now remains for the Commission to act upon his evidence which, we understand, is overwhelming proof of the lawlessness of the factions within Raymond Steel. Let the law be enforced, no matter who the persons implicated might be."

CHAPTER 9

The Reverend Maxwell finished reading his paper and dropped it onto his desk.

"I have to go and see Powers. This is no doubt the result of his promise."

He stood and took hurried steps across the study. His wife stood in the front hall, and asked as he was leaving, "Henry, do you think Jesus would have done that?"

"Done what?" Maxwell stalled.

"What Mr. Powers did."

Maxwell paused a moment. Then he answered slowly, "Yes, I believe He would have. At any rate, Powers must see it that way and each one of us who made the promise understands that he is not deciding Jesus' conduct for anyone else, only for himself."

"What about his family? How will Mrs. Powers and Celia take it?"

"Very hard, I would imagine. That will be Powers' cross in this matter. They will not understand his motive."

A few minutes later, Maxwell pulled into Powers' driveway, and to his relief, the man himself came to the door.

The two men shook hands silently. They instantly understood each other without words. There had never before been such a bond of union between the pastor and one of his members.

"What are you going to do?" Henry Maxwell asked after they had discussed the facts in the case.

"If you mean about finding another job, I have no plans yet. But it shouldn't be difficult, I can find work as a department supervisor in another mill. My family will not suffer, except in a social way."

Powers spoke calmly and sadly. Henry Maxwell did not need to ask him how his wife and daughter felt. He knew well enough that his friend had suffered deepest in this area.

"I will need your help on one important matter," said Powers after a while, "and that is, the work I began at the mill. So far as I know, the company will not object to continuing the lunch speakers' project. One of the greatest contradictions in the corporate world as a whole is that too often, moral values are encouraged among the employees, while the most lawless acts may be committed by management. Of course it stands to reason that in any industry, it would pay to have employees who are family orientated, temperate, honest, and moral. I have no doubt management will continue to permit the use of the lunchroom for this purpose. But, Pastor, what I want you to do is to see that my plan is carried out. Will you? You understand what it was. You made a favorable impression on the employees. Go down there as often as you can. Get Milton Wright to help you provide for the furnishing and expense of the coffee bar and reading tables. Will you do it?"

"Yes, of course," Maxwell replied. He stayed a little longer. Before he left, he and Powers prayed together, and then parted with a silent handshake that seemed to both to be a new token of their Christian discipleship and fellowship.

The pastor of First Church returned home, stirred deeply by the events of the week. Gradually the truth was growing upon him that the pledge to do as Jesus would do was causing a revolution in his church and throughout the city. Every day added to the far-reaching consequences of obedience to that pledge. Maxwell did not pretend to see where all of this would end. He was, in fact, only now beginning to appreciate the enormous impact their simple pledge was destined to make on countless families, not only in Raymond but throughout the country. He thought of Edward Norman and Rachel and Mr. Powers, and the circumstances their actions had already produced. Then he projected ahead to the probable effect if all the persons in First Church who had made the pledge, faithfully kept it. Would they all keep it, or would some turn back when the cost became too great and the cross became too heavy?

The next morning, Maxwell was sitting in his study still pondering this weighty question, when Fred Morris, the president of the church's young adult group, dropped by to see him.

"I suppose I shouldn't trouble you with my problems," said the young man looking at him pensively from across the desk, "but, Pastor, I've been hoping that you might be able to give me some advice."

"I'm glad you came by, Fred. What's on your mind?" Maxwell had known the young man since his first year in the pastorate, and loved and honored him and his family for their consistent, faithful service in the church.

"Well, the fact is, I'm out of a job. You know I've been a reporter at the *Sentinel* since I graduated from college last year. Well, a few days ago, Mr. Burr, my boss at the paper, asked me to change shifts on the news desk. This meant that I would have to work all day Sunday. I refused to make the switch, and Burr fired me. I guess he was in a bad mood or something. He has always treated me well before. Now, do you think Jesus would have done what I did? I ask because the other fellows say I was a fool to refuse to work the new shift. I feel there are times when a Christian may act in a way that seems strange to others. What do you think, Pastor?"

"I think you kept your promise, Fred. I cannot believe Jesus would hold a job that required work every Sunday."

"Thank you, Reverend Maxwell. I felt a little upset about this, but the longer I think it over the better I feel."

Fred Morris rose to go, and his pastor rose and laid a concerned hand on the young man's shoulder.

"What are you going to do, Fred?"

"I don't know yet. I have considered moving to Chicago."

"Why don't you try the *Daily News?*"

"I heard there were no openings, so I didn't bother to go over."

Reverend Maxwell thought for a moment before saying, "Why don't we go over together and see what Mr. Norman has to say."

In a few minutes, Maxwell and Morris were taking the elevator to Norman's executive offices. His secretary ushered them right in and Maxwell quickly stated the purpose of their visit.

"Sure, I can give you a position," said Norman with his penetrating look softened by a smile. "I want newsmen who have the courage to take a moral stand about such things. And there's another reason I would like to hire you. I am planning to make this a newspaper noted for a special breed of reporting. I would be pleased to have someone with your experience and moral conscience. I believe with each story, you will be willing to ask yourself, 'What would Jesus do?'"

Norman hired Morris on the spot and immediately assigned him to a story. As Reverend Maxwell drove back to his office, he felt a strong sense of satisfaction knowing that he had helped someone discover that God honors those who are faithful.

He had intended to go right back to the church but on his way, he passed Milton Wright's office building. His intention was to stop for just a few minutes, but Wright insisted he stay long enough to go over some of his plans. After just a few moments of conversation, Maxwell asked himself if this were truly the Milton Wright he knew to be an eminently practical, businesslike, do-everything-according-to-the-accepted-code-of-the-business world kind of guy. The Wright he knew had always viewed everything first and foremost from the standpoint of, "Will it pay?"

"Reverend Maxwell, since making that pledge in church, I have been forced to totally change my entire approach to business. For the past 20 years, I have been doing a great many things in this store that I know Jesus would not do. But that is a small item compared with the number of things I have begun to believe Jesus would do. In regard to business, my sins of commission have not been as great as those of omission.

"What was the first change you made?" Maxwell asked, forgetting the sermon that was waiting for him back in his study. No matter, his visit with Milton Wright provided more than enough material for two sermons.

"The first change I had to make was in regard to my relationship to my employees," Wright began. "I came to work the day after that unusual

Sunday morning, and I asked myself, 'What would Jesus do in regard to the scores of clerks, bookkeepers, part-timers, and salespeople who work for this company? Would He try to establish some sort of personal relationship with them?' My answer was a resounding 'yes.' Then came the question of what that relationship would be and what it would lead me to do. It seemed clear that I could not answer those questions to my satisfaction without first gathering all my employees and having a talk with them. This is no small undertaking as you would probably guess. So I sent every single one of them an invitation and asked them to meet with me at a warehouse facility I own here in Raymond. The meeting took place last Tuesday night, and a good many things came to light. I tried to talk with my employees as I imagined Jesus would. It was hard work. I have not been in the habit of thinking, much less speaking this way. I know I made some mistakes, but Reverend Maxwell, the effect that meeting had on some of my staff was unbelievable.

"Even while the meeting was in session, I noticed that a lot of people were obviously moved. Some were wiping their eyes; others sat with their heads in their hands thinking. While I spoke I kept asking myself, *What would Jesus do?* and the more I asked, the more I felt the most intimate and loving concern for the men and women who have worked for me all these years. Every day something new comes up that demands a Christlike decision; I find myself in the midst of a complete reevaluation of my companies. I want to zero in on our motives for operations, but truthfully, I have not yet reached definite conclusions in regard to all the details. I'm not used to Jesus' methods, but let me show you something."

Wright punched some information into a computer, and a list appeared on the screen. "I want you to tell me what you think of this. I have sketched out what seems to me to be business principles that Jesus might use to run a company like mine."

WHAT WOULD JESUS DO AS A BUSINESSMAN?

1. Jesus would engage in business for the purpose of glorifying God first and foremost, rather than for the primary purpose of making money.

2. Jesus would never regard the money he made as his own, but as funds entrusted to him for the good of humanity.

3. Jesus' relations with all the persons in his employment would come from a loving and caring heart. His thought for them would always be greater than a desire for worldly success.

4. Jesus would never be involved in any dishonest or questionable act, nor would He in any way take unfair advantage of a fellow businessman.

5. Jesus would allow a spirit of selflessness to direct all decisions.

6. Jesus would extend His righteous plans to His customers as well as the general business world.

Reverend Maxwell read the declaration slowly. It reminded him of his own attempts to verbalize his thoughts of Jesus' probable action.

"Do you believe you can continue to prosper financially while operating according to these principles?"

"I do. Intelligent selflessness ought to be more profitable than intelligent selfishness, don't you think? If my employees feel that they will personally share in the profits and are given a sense of ownership in the company as a whole, won't the results be more care, less waste, more diligence, and more faithfulness?"

"Yes, I think so. However, a good many businessmen will scoff at this, won't they? How will this float in a selfish world that is not concerned with making money based on Christian principles?"

"That complicates my situation, of course."

"But, as I told you, I'm studying my options carefully. I am absolutely convinced that in my place Jesus would be absolutely selfless. He would love all these men and women in His employment. He would consider the main purpose of all business to be mutually beneficial, and He would conduct it all so that God's Kingdom is clearly the first priority. I'll need some time to complete the details."

When Maxwell left, he was profoundly impressed with the revolution that was already gaining momentum. There was no mistaking the fact that Milton Wright had put into place a new relationship with his employees that would soon transform his entire company.

Back in his study, Maxwell prayed that the Holy Spirit, who had already shown Himself strong on behalf of His First Church disciples, would continue to direct them. And with that prayer on his lips and in his heart, he began the preparation of a sermon in which he would address the issues of drugs and other addictive vices, not in some general way but as they specifically affected the city of Raymond. He had never preached in this way before, and yet he was certain that his words would have serious repercussions. As he went on with his work, he preceded every sentence with the question, "Would Jesus say that?" Once in the course of his study, he went down on his knees, a sermon-preparation posture he had not used for years. In his new vision of ministry, he did not dare preach without praying for wisdom. He no longer thought of his dramatic delivery and its effect on his audience. The great question with him now was, "What would Jesus do?"

On Saturday night, Reverend Gray and his wife witnessed some of the most remarkable scenes they had ever known. The meetings increased in intensity as a result of the faithfulness of First Church disciples. A stranger walking through the area during the day would have heard a good deal about the meetings. It cannot be said that up to that Saturday night there had been any appreciable decline in the availability of prostitution or the abuse of drugs and alcohol. The residents and frequenters of the Rectangle district were not ready to acknowledge that the meetings were making any impression on them. Just as in any other characteristic, people sometimes take pride in their "toughness." That was the case in this circumstance. After being pushed off and rejected for so long—treated with disregard—the inhabitants of the Rectangle district were distrustful of any hand extended toward them. Nevertheless, the persistence of the Christian disciples brought with them a power that could not be resisted forever.

Reverend Gray's voice recovered quickly and by Saturday he was able to speak. The fact that he was obliged to use his voice carefully made it necessary for the people to be very quiet if they wanted to hear. Gradually, they came to understand that this man who had been coming and speaking to them these many weeks, giving of his time and strength, had done so in order to bring them a gift—the love of Christ. It had all been done from a heart of love. Tonight the great crowd was as quiet as Reverend Maxwell's sophisticated audiences had ever been. The groups standing in the doorways and out on the sidewalk were larger and the bars were practically empty. The Holy Spirit had come at last, and Gray knew that one of the great prayers of his life was about to be answered.

Rachel's singing was wonderful. The best that Virginia and Jasper had ever heard. They came together again tonight, this time with Dr. West, who had spent all his spare time that week in the Rectangle district providing free medical care for the residents. Virginia was at the piano, and Jasper sat on a front seat looking up at Rachel. The audience leaned forward as one person to hear her sing:

Just as I am, without one plea,
But that Thy blood was shed for me,
And that Thou bidst me come to Thee,
O Lamb of God, I come, I come.

Gray hardly said a word. He stretched out his hand with a gesture of invitation, and down the aisle, broken men and women stumbled toward the platform. One woman who stood close to the piano caught Virginia's attention. The look on the woman's face reminded her of what Jesus must have meant to the sinful woman described in the gospels. Inspired, Virginia left the piano, and went to her. She looked into her face and took her hands in her own. The woman trembled slightly, and then fell to her knees sobbing. After a moment's hesitation, Virginia knelt beside her, and their two heads were bowed close together.

On the floor, across the front of the platform, people had crowded in a double row, most on their knees. Many were crying. A well-dressed man in a business suit pushed through the crowd and knelt beside a drunken man. Rachel Winslow was still singing softly. Turning to one side, she noticed a man dressed in a suit, and was amazed to see that it was Rollin Page! For a moment her voice faltered. Then she went on:

> Just as I am, thou wilt receive,
> Wilt welcome, pardon, cleanse, relieve,
> Because Thy promise I believe,
> O Lamb of God, I come, I come.

The voice was of divine longing, and the Rectangle district had, for the time being, been swept into the harbor of redemptive grace.

CHAPTER 10

Whoever serves me must follow me.
John 12:26

It was nearly midnight before the service in the storefront chapel ended. Reverend Gray stayed up long into Sunday morning, praying and talking with a small group of repentant seekers. Among these new believers was Rollin Page.

Virginia and her uncle went home about eleven o'clock. Jasper Chase and Rachel walked out with them and continued down the street to where their cars were parked. Dr. West climbed into his car, and Rachel left with Jasper.

As the clocks all over Raymond were striking midnight, Jasper Chase sat in his room reviewing the last half hour's events.

He had told Rachel of his love for her, but she had offered him no encouragement that she felt the same for him.

Never had he felt her influence so strongly as he had tonight. While she sang, it seemed to him that there was no one else present, even though the chapel was filled with a crowd of faces. It wasn't just her beauty—there was a glow about her that was very attractive. It was so much more. He knew he had to speak to her when they were alone.

Now that he had spoken, he feared he had misjudged either Rachel or the situation. He had been certain that she was beginning to feel something for him. Rachel knew that she had been the model for the heroine of Jasper's first novel, and he had been the hero. The two characters loved each other. Rachel had not objected and no one else knew about it. That was nearly a year ago.

Tonight, he had openly declared his love. "Rachel," Jasper had said, "I never knew until tonight how much I love you. I can't keep quiet about it any longer."

Rachel had allowed him to speak what was on his heart, and had neither turned her face toward him nor away from him. She looked straight ahead. Her voice was low, but firm as she spoke.

"Why would you bring this up now, after all that we have seen and heard tonight? What's wrong with you?"

"Why—what—" Jasper stammered and then was silent.

Rachel withdrew her arm from his, but still sat near him. Then he cried out in exasperation, "Rachel! Don't you love me? Isn't my love for you as sacred as anything that took place tonight?"

She rode silently for a few blocks. They stopped at a traffic light, and Rachel's face was illuminated by a street lamp. He reached over to take her hand, but she pulled it away and moved a little farther from him.

"No," she finally replied. "There was a time, but everything is different now. You shouldn't have tried to tell me about your feelings now—not after all that happened tonight."

Jasper heard the answer to his declaration in Rachel's response. He could not bring himself to plead with her.

"Maybe sometime in the future . . . ," he began, but she wasn't listening. When they drove into her driveway, Rachel got out of the car without speaking and ran up the walk to her front door.

Now as he replayed the brief but significant scene, he blamed himself for his foolish presumption. He had not taken into consideration Rachel's tense, passionate absorption in the fervent scenes at the chapel. As the clock in the First Church steeple struck one o'clock, Jasper was still at his desk staring at the last page of his unfinished novel.

In the privacy of her room, Rachel faced the experiences of the evening with conflicting emotions. Had she ever loved Jasper Chase? *Yes . . . No. . . .* One moment she felt that her indecision could cost her a lifetime of happiness. A moment later, she felt strangely relieved that she had responded in the way she had. There was, however, one great, overriding emotion that she could not shake off the deep and settled contentment that came as a result of seeing how people in the chapel responded to her singing. The swift, powerful, awesome presence of the Holy Spirit affected her as never before. The moment Jasper spoke her name and she realized that he was telling her of his love, she felt a sudden annoyance that he had failed to respect the supernatural events they had just witnessed. She felt as if it were not the time to be absorbed in anything less than the spirit and glory of those conversions. She had been singing with an anointing that touched the hearts of all those who crowded into the storefront chapel. And there was Jasper Chase, who seemed unmoved by it all, thinking only of his love for her. She was disgusted by his irreverence.

Rachel could not understand why she felt so strongly about the matter. And yet she was convinced that had Jasper chosen not to declare his feelings for her on such an extraordinary night, she might have continued to feel as she always had about him. Had she made a mistake? She went to her desk and took out the manuscript Jasper had given her. Her face deepened with color as she turned to those passages she knew Jasper had written for her. She read them again, but this time they failed to touch her. She gathered the sheets of paper and placed them carefully in a folder.

Her mind continued to be preoccupied with the sights she had witnessed that night at the chapel. Those faces, touched for the first time with the Spirit's glory—with a realization that life can indeed be a wonderful thing after all! The reality of regeneration was revealed in the sight of hurting people kneeling down to give themselves up to a loving God and a life of purity. It was surely a witness to God's involvement in the world! And the face of Rollin Page there with them. She had seen Virginia crying with her arms around her brother just before she left the chapel, and Reverend Gray kneeling close by. She remembered the woman Virginia had taken into her heart and saw her whisper something to her as they walked together to the chapel door. All these scenes played out by the hand of the Holy Spirit in the poorest and most needy area in Raymond, flooded Rachel's mind and heart.

"No! No!" she cried aloud. "He had no right to speak to me in such a way after all that happened! He should have respected the place where my thoughts were—where his thoughts should have been. I am sure I don't love him—not enough to give him my life!"

The people of Raymond awoke Sunday morning with an expanding awareness of the revolution that was taking place in their city. Alexander Powers' action as a result of corruption at the Raymond Steel had created a sensation not only in Raymond but throughout that part of the country. Edward Norman's daily policy changes with respect to his media empire, and specifically the *Daily News* had startled the community and caused more comment than any recent political campaign. Rachel Winslow's singing at the meetings in the Rectangle district had also made a stir inside the city's music community and baffled her friends.

Virginia's presence every night at the chapel, and her absence from her usual circle of influential and fashionable acquaintances, had furnished a great deal of material for gossip. In addition to these issues, which centered around some of Raymond's leading citizens, there had been strange happenings all through the city in many homes, businesses, and social circles. Hundreds of people in Reverend Maxwell's church had now made the pledge to do nothing without first asking, "What would Jesus do?" and the result had been, in many cases, astonishing. The city was stirred as it had never been before. Shortly before the morning service, word had come that there had been 50 conversions resulting from the meetings at the storefront chapel and Rollin Page, well-known to be a playboy, had been one of them.

Under this pressure, it is no wonder that the members of the First Church of Raymond took their seats ready to hear and receive truth. Perhaps nothing had astonished the people more than the great change that had come over their pastor since he had proposed his plan to imitate Jesus and walk in His steps. The dramatic delivery of his sermons no longer impressed them. The self-satisfied, contented, fine figure and refined face in the pulpit had been replaced by an urgency that could not be compared with his previous style. The sermon had become a living message. It was no longer delivered, it was brought to them with love, earnestness, passion, and a humility that expressed genuine enthusiasm for the truth. Reverend Maxwell had become a living channel through which the words of God were spoken. His prayers were unlike any the people had heard before. They were often halting, even grammatically incorrect on occasion, but the people of First Church did not mind. When had he ever forgotten himself so completely in prayer? The needs of his people and his fervent desire to do as His Savior would do rendered him unaware of his occasional mistakes. He had never prayed so effectively as he did now.

There are times when a sermon is powerful because of the conditions that are being addressed, rather than because new and eloquent words and arguments are being presented. Such conditions faced Maxwell this morning as he continued to preach against the evils of drugs and alcohol. He had no new statements to make about the damage done by these evils—no new arguments about the families in Raymond that were being ruined because of them. He offered no startling illustrations of the destructive power of drugs in business and politics. The effect of his message this morning owed its power to the unusual fact that he was preaching about Raymond's drug and alcohol problems at all.

In the ten years that he had been pastor of First Church, Henry Maxwell had never mentioned these evils. He had never addressed them as enemies—not only of the poor, but also of the affluent. He had never before stressed that this enemy had invaded businesses, families, and incredibly, the church itself. He spoke with a freedom that revealed his conviction that in this situation, Jesus would speak as he was speaking now. At the close of the message, he pleaded with people to remember the lives that had been transformed during the meetings in the Rectangle district.

The election of city officers was near at hand. The restriction of liquor, drugs, and gambling would be important issues in the campaign. What would happen to those changed lives if the people of the First Church of Raymond refused to insist that City Hall take its responsibilities more seriously? It was time to tell legislators that the people of Raymond demanded the enforcement of laws dealing with the city's rampant social ills.

Was there not one word to be said by Christians, committed businessmen, teachers, the clergy, or the average citizen, in favor of stamping out these evils in the city of Raymond? Could they not see that fighting for the election of concerned and honorable men and women in city offices was one of the most Christian acts of all?

Reverend Maxwell pointed out that they had prayed God would make Raymond better, but their votes and actions had actually been on the side of the enemies of Jesus. Would Jesus do this? What disciple could imagine Him refusing to suffer or to take up His cross in this matter? How much had the members of First Church ever suffered in an attempt to imitate Jesus? Was Christian discipleship a matter of conscience or custom or tradition? Where did the suffering come in? Was it necessary in order to follow Jesus' steps to go up to Calvary as well as the Mount of Transfiguration?

Maxwell's appeal was stronger at this point than he realized. It is not too much to say that the people's interest reached its highest point right there. The imitation of Jesus which had begun with the church's volunteers, was working like a leavening agent. Maxwell would have been amazed if he could have measured the extent of desire on the part of his people to take up the cross. Even before he reached the close of his message, many men and women seated on First Church pews were declaring, "I want to do those things that will cost me something." Truly, no appeal is quite so powerful in the end as the call: "Come and suffer."

The service was over, the great audience had gone, and Maxwell again faced the company gathered in the side chapel. He had asked everyone to remain who had made the pledge of discipleship, and any others who wished to be included. Such a meeting after the service seemed a necessity. Reverend Maxwell felt his heart tremble as he entered the room and faced his people. There were several hundred people present. The Holy Spirit had never felt so near. Maxwell looked around for Jasper Chase, but all the others were present. He asked Milton Wright to pray. The air seemed to be charged with divine possibilities. Who could resist such a baptism of power? How had they lived all these years without it?

The energized group counseled together and had prayer in which God's presence was manifested in many ways. There were tears and pleadings for power—there was an unction that old-time preachers used to talk about. Reverend Maxwell dated from that meeting many uncommon events that later became part of the history of First Church and of Raymond. When they finally went home, all were impressed with the glory of the Spirit's power.

CHAPTER 11

Donald Marsh, president of Lincoln College, offered to drive his pastor home after the service. Mary Maxwell was making a hospital call with the car.

"I have reached one conclusion, Pastor," admitted Marsh, speaking slowly. "I have found my cross and it's a heavy one, but I shall never be satisfied until I take it up and carry it." Maxwell was silent as the president continued.

"Your sermon this morning made clear to me what I have long felt I should do. Since I made my pledge, I have repeatedly asked the question 'What would Jesus do in my place?' I'm afraid that there are times when I have conned myself into believing that He would simply go on as I have done—attending to the duties of my administrative work and teaching classes in ethics and philosophy. In spite of my busyness, I have not been able to avoid the feeling that Christ would do something more. I guess I have known all along what that *something* is. The problem is that I don't want to do it. It will cause me genuine suffering, and I dread it with all my heart and soul. You may be able to guess what it is."

"Yes, I think I know. It is my cross too. I would almost rather do anything else."

Donald Marsh looked surprised, then relieved. He spoke with great conviction.

"Pastor, you and I belong to a class of professionals who have always avoided politics. Typically, we live in a rather closed environment of literature and scholarly pursuits, doing work we enjoy and shrinking back from the disagreeable issues faced by average citizens. I confess with shame that I have purposely avoided my personal responsibility to this city. I understand that our officials at City Hall are for the most part a corrupt, unprincipled group of people, and that they are controlled in large part by kickbacks and influence peddling from gambling interests, the liquor lobby, tobacco interests, and worse. Yet all these years, I, along with almost every teacher in the college, have been satisfied to let other people dirty their hands by speaking out against corrupt and self-seeking politicians. I'm afraid that I have lost touch with the real world.

"I feel I have avoided a truthful answer to the question, 'What would Jesus do?' I realize that if I am to make good on my pledge, I cannot continue this way. It seems to me that it is my duty to play a part in the upcoming election. I hope to become involved in the primaries, and throw the weight of my influence, whatever it is, toward the nomination and election of worthy candidates. Now frankly, Reverend Maxwell, I would sooner stand before a firing squad than do this. I would give almost anything to be able to say, 'I do not believe Jesus would do anything of the sort.' But I am persuaded that He would. This is where the suffering comes for me. I loath politics. It would suit me just fine to remain quietly ensconced in my scholastic life, but the call has come to me so clearly that I cannot turn my back. It is as if Jesus Himself is saying, 'Donald Marsh, follow Me. Do your duty as a citizen of Raymond at the point where your citizenship will cost you something.' Pastor, this is my cross, I must take it up or face my disobedience to God."

"You have spoken for me also," replied Maxwell with a thoughtful smile. "Why should I, simply because I am a minister, shelter myself behind my refined, sensitive feelings, and like a coward refuse to do my duty as a citizen? I'm not used to the ways of Raymond's political life. I have never made an effort to nominate good leaders. There are hundreds of other ministers in this city, just like me, who have never become involved in the political process here in Raymond, except from our pulpits.

"So, 'what would Jesus do?' I am now at a point where, like you, I can answer that question in only one way. My duty is obvious, and it will require sacrifice. In comparison, my ministerial work and all my little trials and self-sacrifices seem like nothing. I could live in the Rectangle district for the rest of my life and work in the slums for a bare living, and I could enjoy it more than the thought of plunging into a fight against corruption in this city. It would cost me less. But, like you, I have been unable to shake off my responsibility. The answer to the question 'What would Jesus do?' in this case leaves me with no peace except when I say, Jesus would have me act like a Christian citizen.

"Mr. Marsh, as you have said, it is time for us to recognize that we have acted like political cowards, ignorantly or selfishly avoiding the sacred duties of citizenship. Certainly in our age Jesus would not do that. We can do no less than take up our crosses, and follow Him."

The two men rode awhile in silence before Marsh added, "Just the same, we shouldn't feel that we are required to act alone in this matter. There are plenty of others who have made the pledge, and if nothing else, there will be strength in our numbers. I suggest that we take it upon ourselves to organize the Christian forces of Raymond for battle. We certainly should be able to enter the primaries with a force capable of more than a simple protest against corruption. Let's plan a campaign that means something because it is organized for righteousness. Jesus would use great wisdom in this matter, and I am certain He would go about it in the right way. Whatever we do, we must approach it bravely and with conviction."

Sitting in front of the Maxwell's home, they continued to talk, then agreed to meet again the next day to develop their plans. The primaries were approaching and political rumblings were beginning to be noticed throughout Raymond. The usual system of nominating candidates in the state required that names be submitted at a public meeting at the courthouse.

The citizens of Raymond are unlikely to forget that meeting. It was so unlike any political gathering they had ever experienced. The offices of mayor, city council, police chief, city clerk, and city treasurer were challenged.

The *Daily News* ran a full account of the nominations in the evening issue of its Saturday edition, and in his editorial column, Edward Norman spoke with a directness and conviction that the people of Raymond were learning to respect, because it was so evidently sincere and unselfish. A part of that editorial is also a part of this story:

> It is safe to say that never before in the history of Raymond has there been a nominating meeting like the one at the courthouse last night. It was, first of all, a complete surprise to the city's incumbent politicians who have been in the habit of carrying on the affairs of the city as if they owned them. The assembly room was filled to overflowing with Raymond's citizenship, most of whom had never before taken part in the city's affairs. For the most part, these political "neophytes" controlled the discussions from the outset. They were responsible for the nomination of many excellent candidates.
>
> Last night's nominating primary was a tremendous lesson in good citizenship.

President Marsh of Lincoln College, who has never before entered a city primary, and whose face was not even known to the ward politicians, delivered one of the best speeches ever heard in Raymond. Reaction to the president by the incumbent political clique was, to a person, one of incredulity. "Who is he?" they asked. The consternation deepened as the primary proceeded and it became evident that the old ringleaders were outnumbered.

Among the professionals participating in this exercise of the democratic process were the Reverend Henry Maxwell of First Church; businessmen Milton Wright and Alexander Powers; educators Timothy Brown, Jackson Willard, and Alexander Park of Lincoln College; and Dr. Charles West. Other clergy present included Reverend George Main of Pilgrim Church, Reverend Dean Ward of Holy Trinity, and scores of other well-known business and professional people, most of whom are members of local churches. It did not take long to see that these individuals had all come with one purpose in mind: to nominate the best candidates possible. Many of those nominated had never before been seen in a primary. They were complete strangers to the political powers that be. Despite their seeming lack of experience in the political arena, these individuals were able to fill the entire ticket with candidates sympathetic to their views. This was evidently the result of the mobilization of an organized and united front. As soon as it became plain that the primary was out of their control, Raymond's politicos withdrew and promptly nominated their own ticket.

The *Daily News* wishes to call to the attention of Raymond's decent citizens that this second ticket bears the names of a cartel of gambling, alcohol, and tobacco interests. It appears that the lines have been distinctly drawn between the elements of vice and corruption in our city's government and those who are insisting on the election of a clean, honest, capable, and businesslike city administration.

It is not necessary to remind the people of Raymond that the question of liquor licensing will be addressed in this important upcoming election. It is, in the opinion of this newspaper, the most important question on the ticket. We have reached a crisis in the affairs of our city government, and it is time to face these types of difficult issues squarely. We cannot afford to leave in place a government fraught with corruption and incompetence. As President Marsh said in his speech, "It is time for the good citizens of Raymond to enforce a new order, ridding our city of political corruption and immoral vice. It is time to take up the fight through the power of the ballot."

The management of the *Daily News* is positively and without reservation on the side of this new movement. We shall henceforth do all in our power to drive out vice and corruption and destroy their political strength. We shall advocate the election of the candidates nominated by the moral and upright citizens of Raymond to stand with President Marsh and those who have committed themselves to the long-needed reform in our city.

President Marsh read the editorial and thanked God for Edward Norman. At the same time, he understood well enough that every other paper and television station in Raymond would almost certainly take another view. He did not under-estimate the importance and gravity of the battle that now faced Raymond, but he also knew that the *Daily News* had lost a large number of readers since Norman's decision to follow in the steps of Jesus. So, the question was, would the spiritual people of Raymond stand by the cause? Would they make it possible for Norman to run a daily newspaper according to the ideals of Jesus Christ? Or would those who profit from crime, scandal, and political partisanship be able to defeat this noble endeavor? That was in fact the question Edward Norman was asking himself, even as he was writing his outspoken Saturday editorial. He knew well enough that the action suggested in his piece would come at a great personal cost. And still, as he put his pen to the paper, he asked another question, "What would Jesus do?" That question had now become the guiding force of his life.

For the first time in its history, Raymond saw its professional community, made up of teachers, college professors, doctors, the clergy, and others take political action that would put them squarely in the midst of controversy. President Marsh acknowledged with regret that never before had he known what civic responsibility could accomplish. Based on his experience with the meeting at City

Hall, he created for himself and his college a new definition of the worn phrase, "the scholar in politics." The element of suffering would have to be understood as part and parcel of the process. Sacrifice would now become a factor in every political accomplishment.

In the Rectangle district, the tide of spiritual victory showed no signs of ebbing. The meetings in the storefront chapel continued and Rachel and Virginia attended every night. In light of it all, Virginia was rapidly reaching a conclusion with respect to her money. She and Rachel agreed that if Jesus had a vast sum of money at His disposal, He might do with it as Virginia planned. There was of course no one fixed way in which Christians were obliged to use their money. The guiding principle for its regulation seemed to be selflessness and responsibility.

Meanwhile, the Spirit continued to be manifest night after night. Each week brought with it miracles as great as walking on the sea or feeding the multitude with a few loaves and fishes. For what greater miracle is there than seeing hurting lives changed and lost souls repentant? The transformation of these down-and-outers into praying, believing, victorious lovers of Christ, struck Rachel and Virginia with the feeling that people may have had when they saw Lazarus walk out of the tomb. It was an experience full of profound excitement for them.

Rollin Page came to all the meetings. There was no doubt that a significant change had come over him. Rachel had not yet spoken much with him. He was quiet and seemed to be thinking all the time. Certainly he was not the same person. He talked more with Reverend Gray than with anyone else. He did not avoid Rachel, but appeared to shrink from any appearance of trying to renew his acquaintance with her. Rachel found it difficult to tell him how excited she was to see his new life beginning. Rollin had not forgotten Rachel or the other people in his life, but he was not yet able to fit his new identity into those relationships.

The end of the week found the residents of the Rectangle district struggling with two mighty opposing forces. The Holy Spirit was battling with all His supernatural strength against the evils which had so long enslaved them. If the Christian people of Raymond could only realize what the contest meant to these newly awakened souls, it did not seem possible that the candidates on the Christian ticket could lose. But that remained to be seen. In the meantime, the reality of life in the Rectangle district—the horror of the daily surroundings of these new believers burnt their way into Virginia and Rachel's hearts. Every night as they drove uptown to their beautiful, comfortable homes, they felt all the more burdened for the circumstances of those they left behind.

"A good many of these converts will go back to their old lives," Reverend Gray had said with a sadness too deep for tears. "You can't escape it; environment has a great deal to do with the development of character. It stands to reason that these people can't live in the midst of alcohol and drug abuse, illicit sex, and gambling without being affected by them. Some will not be able to resist the lure of these vices that beckon from nearly every window, doorway, and curbside. Oh Lord, how long will Christians continue to support, by their silence and their ballots, the slavery that is still rampant in the country?"

Reverend Gray asked the question without much hope for an immediate answer. Granted, there was a ray of hope in the events of the primary meeting, but the lasting results could not be anticipated. The lobbies for alcohol and tobacco were organized, alert, aggressive, roused into battle formation by recent events. Those who dealt in drugs, gambling, and prostitution were equally prepared. Out-of-town interests that stood to lose their strongholds if the Christian ticket won election were pouring huge sums of money into the campaigns of their sympathizers. Would Christians act as a united force against these special interest groups, or would they be divided as a result of compromise and selfish motives? That remained to be seen.

Saturday afternoon as Virginia stepped into her car on her way to meet with Rachel, a small foreign sports car with the top down pulled into the drive. Virginia climbed out of the driver's seat and greeted three of her friends. They had come for a visit and wanted Virginia to go for a ride with them. The plan was to explore a new shopping mall that had just opened in downtown Raymond.

"Where have you been, Virginia?" one of the young women asked playfully. "Are you involved with someone and too busy to tell your friends?" The woman behind the wheel spoke up, "A little bird told us you had gone into show business. What can you tell us about that?"

Virginia laughed, but after a moment's hesitation, she told them about her experiences in the Rectangle district's storefront chapel. Her friends were fascinated and curious about her new found interest.

"Tell you what, ladies, instead of yet another round of shopping, let's go 'slumming' with Virginia this afternoon. I've never even been to the Rectangle district, but I've heard there's plenty to see," one of the friends said with a wink. "Virginia, you should know your way around by now. You can be our guide! What do ya say? Sounds like real fun to me."

Virginia was angry, and her first thought was to flatly refuse the sarcastic offer. But when the other two women chimed in with what seemed to be genuine interest, Virginia began to see an opportunity in her friends' idle curiosity. What an ideal time for them to see the plight of those less fortunate than themselves.

"Sure, let's go!" Virginia declared, climbing into the backseat.

CHAPTER 12

*For I have come to turn "a man against
his father, a daughter against her mother,
a daughter-in-law against her
mother-in-law—a man's enemies
will be the members of his own household."*
Matthew 10:35-36

*Be imitators of God, therefore, as dearly loved
children and live a life of love, just as Christ
loved us and gave himself up for us as a
fragrant offering and sacrifice to God.*
Ephesians 5:1-2

"Maybe we should take some guys along for protection," commented one of the women with a nervous laugh. "It really isn't safe down there, you know."

"There's no danger," said Virginia boldly.

"Is it true that your brother Rollin got converted down there?" asked the first woman, looking at Virginia curiously. It occurred to her that all three of her friends were looking at her as if she were acting quite strangely.

"Yes, he certainly did."

"I understand he is going around to the places where he used to hang out talking with his friends."

"I hear he's trying to preach to them. Isn't that a hoot?" said the driver.

Virginia did not respond. She could tell that the women were beginning to feel nervous as the silver blue car turned into a side street leading to the Rectangle district. With each passing block, they seemed to grow more apprehensive. The sights and smells and sounds of the area had become familiar to Virginia, but they struck a note of fear in these refined women. As they drove further into the heart of the district, the Rectangle, with its ragged inhabitants, crumbling buildings, dirty little children, and drunks seemed to stare with one huge, bleary, booze-soaked countenance at the conspicuous car with its fashionably dressed passengers. "Slumming" had never been a fad with Raymond society, and this was perhaps the first time that the two social orders had confronted each other in this way. The women felt that instead of satisfying their own curiosity, they had become the object of curiosity for others. They quickly lost their enthusiasm for expedition into foreign soil.

"Let's go back. I've seen enough," said the woman who sat next to Virginia in the backseat.

Just at that moment, they pulled up alongside one of the Rectangle's many bars. The street was narrow and crowded with pedestrians Suddenly, out of the bar door, a young woman reeled, singing in a drunken stupor, "Just as I am, without one plea, and that Thy blood. . . ." As the car crept slowly past, the woman raised her face so that Virginia was able to see it very clearly. It was the face of the woman who had knelt beside her in the storefront chapel, sobbing and repentant.

"Stop!" cried Virginia, to the woman behind the wheel. The car came to a jerking halt, and in a moment, she was out and on her way to the woman's side.

"Loreen!" Virginia cried out, taking her arm. As she looked into Virginia's face, her own was frozen by of look of utter horror. Virginia's friends in the car were struck with helpless astonishment. A bartender came to the door of his establishment and stood looking on with his arms folded across his broad expanse. Others peering from windows, tenement steps, the filthy sidewalk, the gutter, and the street paused, and with undisguised wonder stared at the two women. The warm sun of spring poured over the scene with a mellow light. Virginia had never heard the Rectangle district so silent. Every eye was on her and Loreen.

When Virginia jumped from the car and grabbed Loreen's arm, she had no idea what she would do or what the consequences of her action would be. She simply saw a face that a few nights earlier, had been a radiant reflection of God's love, but now mirrored the soul of one slipping back into a hell of shame and hopelessness. In the split second before she jumped from the car and grabbed the women's arm, she had asked only one question, "What would Jesus do?" The question that now, as with many others, had become a habit of life.

Virginia took in the cruelty of the scene around her as she steadied the drunken woman. Suddenly, she thought of her friends in the car.

"Go ahead without me," she called out to them. "I'm going to help my friend get home."

The girl behind the wheel gasped at the notion that Virginia would refer to this miserable person as her "friend." She said nothing. In fact, all the women were rendered speechless by Virginia's incredible act.

"I said, go on without me," Virginia repeated. As the driver started the car, one of the women leaned out and called to her.

"Can't we—that is—do you want our help? Couldn't you—"

"No, no!" exclaimed Virginia. "You can't help me. Thanks anyway."

The car pulled away and Virginia was suddenly alone in the street with her needy friend. The crowd around them seemed sympathetic. They were not all cruel or brutal. The Holy Spirit had softened a good many hearts in the past few weeks.

"Where does she live?" asked Virginia.

No one answered, and for the first time it crossed her mind that this young woman had no place to go. The woman suddenly pulled her arm from Virginia's grasp so violently that Virginia was almost thrown to the ground.

"Don't touch me! Leave me alone! Can't you see I'm not worth saving," she cried out hoarsely. The woman turned and pointed a shaking finger at the bar owner, "He owns me. Don't you understand that!" she cried. Nervous laughter broke out in the crowd as they witnessed this unusual scene. Virginia took Loreen's hand in hers, and then put her arm around her.

"Loreen," she said firmly, "you're coming home with me. You do not belong to that man or anyone else. You belong to Jesus and He will save you. Come on now. Let's go."

The woman suddenly collapsed into sobs.

Virginia looked around again. "Where does Reverend Gray live?" she asked. She knew that the evangelist stayed somewhere near the chapel. A number of people offered directions.

"Come, Loreen, I want you to go with me to Reverend Gray's," she said, holding tight to the trembling woman, who continued to moan and sob.

When they reached the Grays' temporary residence, a woman answered Virginia's knock and told her that both Reverend and Mrs. Gray were out and would not be back until six o'clock.

Virginia had planned to do nothing more than make an appeal to the Grays to take Loreen in until she could sober up and find a safe place to stay. Now she found herself at a loss to know exactly how to proceed. Loreen sank down stupidly on the steps and buried her face in her arms. Virginia eyed the miserable figure with a feeling that she feared would soon grow into disgust.

What was to stop her from taking Loreen home with her? Why shouldn't this needy, homeless woman be given refuge in Virginia's own home instead of being consigned to a shelter or hospital? Virginia really knew very little about homeless shelters. She knew that there were two or three located somewhere in Raymond, but she was doubtful that they would take someone in Loreen's condition. Whatever the case, the question right now seemed to be, "What would Jesus do with Loreen?" That was what Virginia faced.

"Loreen, come on, you're going home with me. We'll call a cab."

The shaky young woman staggered to her feet and, to Virginia's surprise, offered no resistance. She had expected a stubborn refusal to move. Virginia asked the woman inside to call for a cab, and as soon as it arrived, she pushed Loreen inside. "Where to?" the driver asked. Virginia was painfully aware of the cab driver's quizzical stare in the rearview mirror, but her primary concern at that moment was the approaching scene with her grandmother.

Loreen was nearly sober now. But she was weak from hunger and exhaustion. Virginia had to hold on to her. Virginia breathed a sigh of relief as the cab pulled into the drive and stopped, and then steeled herself again as they reached the side door. She prayed under her breath as she put the key in the lock and felt strengthened for whatever obstacles she might now be asked to face.

Mrs. Page emerged from the library just in time to see Virginia step into the hall, supporting Loreen, who stared stupidly at the luxury around her.

"Grandmother," Virginia spoke without hesitation, "I have brought one of my friends from the Rectangle district. She is in trouble and has no place to go so I brought her back here to rest and sort out her options."

Mrs. Page glanced from her granddaughter to Loreen in astonishment.

"Did you say this person is one of your friends?" she asked in a less than cordial voice.

"Yes, that's what I said." Virginia's face flushed, but she seemed to recall a verse that Reverend Gray had used for one of his recent sermons, *Jesus was a friend of publicans and sinners.* Surely, Jesus would do what she had done.

"Do you know who this woman is?" asked Mrs. Page, in an angry whisper as she stepped closer to Virginia.

"I know that she needs my help," Virginia countered. She is homeless and in trouble. But she is also a child of God. I have seen her on her knees praying. And I have seen the long arms of hell reaching out to snatch her back. By the grace of God, I feel that the least I can do is offer her a helping hand. Grandmother, we call ourselves Christians, can we do less than help her?"

Mrs. Page glared at Virginia and clenched her fists. All this was contrary to all the rules of conduct she had ever known. How could she be expected to take in a person off the street? Surely this action would bring little more than criticism and a loss of standing in the community. To Mrs. Page, society represented more than the church or any other institution. It was a power that must be feared and obeyed. The loss of its goodwill was a loss more to be dreaded than anything except the loss of wealth itself.

The matron stood erect and stern and confronted Virginia, who placed her arm about Loreen and calmly looked her grandmother in the face.

"You will not do this, Virginia! You can send her to a homeless shelter or some such thing, but she cannot possibly stay here. I have no objection to covering her expenses, but we simply cannot take in such a person."

"Grandmother, I don't want to do anything that displeases you, but I will not send Loreen to a shelter. You must allow her to stay here tonight and longer if that becomes necessary."

"Then you can suffer the consequences! I will not stay in the same house with a miserable—" Madam Page lost her self-control. Virginia stopped her before she could speak the next word.

"Grandmother, this is my house. It is also your home as long as you choose to remain. But in this circumstance, I must act as I believe Jesus would if He were in my place. I am willing to deal with the ridicule of our neighbors, but I feel that Loreen's present needs are more important than the opinions of others."

"I will not stay here, then!" Mrs. Page declared, abruptly turning away and walking to the end of the hall. She paused a moment, and then came back to face her granddaughter.

"I want you to remember that you have driven your grandmother out of your home in favor of a drunken woman." Then without waiting for Virginia to reply, she turned again and went upstairs. Virginia called the housekeeper and soon Loreen was being cared for. During the brief scene in the hall, Loreen had held on to Virginia with such force that her arm was sore from the pressure of the woman's fingers.

Virginia did not know whether her grand-mother would leave the house or not. She had plenty of resources of her own, and was perfectly healthy, vigorous, and capable of caring for herself. She had sisters and brothers living in the South and was in the habit of spending several weeks of the year with them. Virginia was not anxious about her welfare. Nevertheless, the encounter had been a painful one. Going over it in her room before she went down to tea, she found little cause for regret. "What would Jesus do?" There was no question in her mind that she had done the right thing. If her action had been a mistake, it was one of judgment rather than intent.

CHAPTER 13

Toward the end of the afternoon, Virginia went downstairs, but her grandmother was nowhere to be found. A few minutes later, Rollin came in and broke the news that he had been at the airport dropping off some friends and happened to see the chauffeur unloading her luggage. "She's off to Atlanta," he reported, "and she's not very happy. She told me what happened."

Virginia and Rollin comforted each other.

For the first time since his conversion, Virginia realized how much her brother's changed life meant to her. "Rollin," she asked, "Was I wrong?"

"No, sis, you did the right thing. Even though Grandmother's behavior is painful for us, this helpless woman owes her safety and salvation to your personal care. What else could you do? What's really painful, Virginia, is to realize that for all these years, we have been so selfish—we've enjoyed our beautiful home and all these luxuries, but we have forgotten that there are multitudes of people just like this woman! I am convinced that if Jesus were in our places, He would do exactly what you have done."

And so Rollin comforted and counseled Virginia that evening. It almost overwhelmed her when she considered what had now happened as a result of her pledge to follow Jesus' example. However, nothing affected her so powerfully as the change in Rollin's life. He was indeed a new person in Christ. Old things were passed away. All things in Him had become new.

At Virginia's request, Dr. West came that evening to do everything necessary for Loreen. He confirmed that her greatest needs at present were quiet care, and love. Virginia chose a beautiful room with a picture of Jesus on the wall opposite the bed in hope that this pleasant environment would encourage her to rest and regain her strength. Meanwhile, Virginia moved nearer the great heart of Christ.

The Rectangle populace awaited the municipal election with great interest. Reverend Gray and his wife wept and prayed over their converts, who, confronted daily with enticing evils and wearied by the struggle, often returned to their old lives.

The follow-up meeting at First Church was eagerly attended. Reverend Maxwell entered the chapel the Sunday after the week of the successful primary election meeting and was enthusiastically greeted by a crowd that stretched literally from wall to wall. He noted that Jasper Chase was again absent, but he was pleased that all the others were present. The group seemed drawn closely together by a bond of common fellowship. To those gathered, it was understood that the Spirit of Jesus was the spirit of open and frank confession. To Edward Norman it seemed the most natural thing in the world to update the rest of the company about his latest newspaper exploits.

"The fact is," admitted Norman, " I have lost a great deal of money in the past three weeks. I'm not sure exactly how much, but I do know that I am losing a large number of subscribers every day."

"What do the subscribers give as their reason for dropping the paper?" asked Reverend Maxwell.

"I've heard a good many different reasons. Some say they want a paper that prints all the news; meaning crime details, lottery results, casino information, sensational gossip, scandals, and the like. Others object to my decision to discontinue the Sunday edition. I have lost thousands of subscribers for that reason alone, although I have made satisfactory arrangements with many of the old subscribers by giving them even more in the Saturday evening edition than they formerly had in the Sunday issue.

"My greatest loss has come from a falling off in advertising revenues, and the stand I have taken on political issues. The majority of my subscribers are intensely political. I may as well tell you that if I continue to pursue as I honestly believe Jesus would pursue, the *Daily News* will not be able to pay its operating expenses—except that is, for one factor."

He paused a moment and the room was very quiet. Virginia seemed especially interested. She soon found that Norman's words mirrored her own thinking.

"That one factor is the Christian community in Raymond. Let's say the newspaper has heavy losses because the people who do not care for a daily with Christian values choose to drop their subscriptions. I am wondering if there are enough genuine Christians in Raymond to support a paper edited as Jesus probably would have edited it? Or are the habits of Raymond's church folks so firmly fixed on yellow journalism that they will not take a newspaper unless it is largely without a Christian and moral purpose?"

The assembled group didn't move. They hung on Norman's words.

"Let me say off the record to you my friends and fellow disciples that because of recent complications in my business affairs, I have lost a large part of my fortune. I was committed to applying the rule of Jesus' probable conduct to certain transactions with other men who did not apply this rule. The result has been the loss of a great deal of money. As I understand, the pledge we made did not include the proviso, 'Will it pay?' All of our actions were to be based on the solitary question: 'What would Jesus do?' Acting on that and that alone, I have lost nearly all the money I have accumulated from my paper and other communication enterprises. It is not necessary for me to go into detail. There was no question in my mind from the beginning that the course of action we have chosen could cost many of us a vast sum of money. I mention my loss to you because I have the fullest confidence in the ultimate success of a daily paper based on Christian values. I am willing to put my entire fortune into the paper in order to achieve that goal. Yet unless the Christian people of Raymond, the church members and professing disciples, are willing to support the paper with subscriptions and advertising, I cannot continue its publication."

As Virginia listened to Mr. Norman's words, a question took form in her mind.

"Mr. Norman, do you mean that a Christian newspaper needs to be endowed with a large sum of money like a Christian college in order to make it succeed?"

"That is exactly what I mean. My plan for the *Daily News* is to include such a variety of materials written and presented in such a powerful and truly interesting way that it would more than make up for those questionable elements that have been omitted. This plan calls for a very large outlay of money. I am very confident that such a daily newspaper can be made to be financially profitable if it is planned in this way. But it will take a large sum of money to undertake these plans."

"How much money are you thinking about?" asked Virginia quietly.

Edward Norman looked at her keenly, and his face flushed a moment as it occurred to him what she might have in mind. He had known her when she was a little girl carrying her Bible into Sunday school, and he had worked closely with her father in years gone by.

"I would say that the investment of a few million dollars to establish such a newspaper in our city would be well spent," he answered, his voice trembling slightly.

"Then," said Virginia, speaking with finality, "I am ready to put that kind of money into the paper on this condition. The paper must not waver from its present Christian editorial policy."

"Thank God!" exclaimed Reverend Maxwell softly. Mr. Norman could barely believe what he had just heard. The entire group was looking at Virginia and waiting, for it seemed she had more to say.

"Dear friends," she went on, "I don't want any of you to give me credit for any act of great generosity. I have come to realize that the money which I have called my own is not mine, but God's. If I, as His steward, see some wise way to invest His money, it's not an occasion for pride on my part, nor should anyone thank me; I am only being honest in the administration of the funds He's asked me to care for to His glory. I've been working on this very plan for some time. The fact is, when we take on the enemy here in Raymond—and, frankly, it's my belief that the struggle has just begun—we will need the *Daily News* to communicate truth in the heat of battle. We know that the city's other papers will be controlled by alcohol and gambling interests, not to mention prostitution and drugs.

"It would be surrendering to the enemy if we allow the *News* to fail. I have great confidence in Mr.

Norman's ability as a successful communicator. I have not seen his plans, but I share his confidence that the paper can be successful if it is carried forward on a large enough scale. So that is my reason for putting God's money into this powerful media channel for the sake of doing as Jesus would do. If we can keep the paper going for one year, the money will be well used. Remember, I deserve no thanks. What have I done with God's money all these years but gratify my own selfish, personal desires? What can I do with the rest of it but try to make some reparation for what I have stolen from God? That is the way I look at it now. I believe it is what Jesus would do."

An unseen, yet distinctly felt, wave of God's presence swept through the chapel. No one was able to speak. Reverend Maxwell felt a strange sensation that they had traveled out of the present back into the Book of Acts. He was aware of a Spirit of fellowship that flowed freely between believers in a way that the First Church of Raymond had never known before—until now. There was an unspoken comradeship such as they had never known before. It was present with them while Virginia was speaking, and during the silence that followed. If one of them had been asked to describe or define this new closeness, that person might have said something like this, "If in the course of my obedience to my pledge, I should meet with loss or trouble in the world, I can depend on this part of the Body, who, along with me, has made the pledge to do all things by the rule, 'What would Jesus do?'"

Perhaps this is what the first century disciples experienced. Perhaps this is what gave them confidence and helped them to face loss and martyrdom with courage and even joy.

Before they went their separate ways, members of the group lingered to share confidential stories like that of Edward Norman. Some of the young men and women told of job losses due to their honest obedience to the pledge.

Alexander Powers spoke briefly of the fact that the commission had promised to take action on his evidence at the earliest date possible.

It was a significant fact that, since resigning his position, neither his wife nor daughter had been seen in public. No one no matter how sympathetic could comprehend the price he had paid through the estrangement of his family and the common misunderstanding of motive. Many of the disciples present in the chapel meeting carried similar burdens—things they could not freely discuss. Because he knew his people, Reverend Maxwell knew with certainty that obedience to their pledge had produced suffering in the hearts of many who failed to understand their conviction. For some, it meant the introduction of strife and division in their homes and on their jobs. He also knew that a person's worst foes can often be those of his own household, especially when the rule of Christ is honored by some and disregarded by others. Jesus can be a great divider in life.

CHAPTER 14

By far the overriding emotion experienced by the group in the chapel that day was the tide of fellowship that swept through the room. Reverend Maxwell did not know what would happen as a result of this bonding experience, but he was not unduly alarmed by it. With growing wonder, he watched their responses to the consequences of the seemingly simple pledge they had made. The results of that pledge could now be seen throughout the city. By the end of the year, it would be impossible to accurately measure its influence.

One practical form of this growing sense of fellowship could be seen in the encouragement Edward Norman received with regard to his paper. At the close of the meeting, his fellow disciples flocked around him. His appeal for help from the Christian community in Raymond was fully understood by this company of believers. The value of such a paper in their homes on behalf of godliness and good citizenship could not be minimized. Now it remained to be seen what the paper could do in the light of Virginia's unexpected endowment. Though it still was true, as Norman insisted, that money alone could not make the paper successful, still it had to have the support and sympathy of the Christians in Raymond before it could be counted as a great force in the city.

The week that followed that Sunday's meeting was one of great excitement in Raymond. It was election week. President Marsh, true to his promise, took up his cross and carried it, but not without a few groans and even tears. His deepest convictions were affected by this action. He had torn himself away from years of scholarly seclusion with a pain and anguish that cost him more than anything he had ever done as a follower of Christ. Standing beside him were a few of the college professors who had also made the pledge in First Church. Their experience and suffering were also great. The same was true of Reverend Maxwell, who plunged into the horror of this fight against vice and corruption with a near dread of each day's new encounter. Never before had he borne such a cross. There were times when he staggered under it. During those brief times when he took a pause from his work to sit and have a cup of coffee with Mary, or when he sought the solitude of his study, the realization of what he had undertaken would break upon him, and he would feel as if he had marched unsuspectingly into unknown horrors. He was not a coward, but he felt the panic and dread that most people feel when duty is suddenly thrust upon them. A duty which carries with it action so unfamiliar that it reveals inexperience and ushers in the fear of humiliation.

By the time election day finally came, the excitement had risen to a high pitch. Even though it was Saturday, an attempt was made to close all the bars in town in an effort to calm boiling tempers. That strategy was not successful, however. Tensions were particularly overwhelming in the Rectangle district where residents boiled and heaved and cursed and insisted on presenting their worst possible side to the city as a whole.

Evangelist Gray continued his meetings during election week, and the results were even greater than he had dared to hope. By the time election day came, it seemed to him that the forces of good and evil were quickly approaching a confrontation. As the crowds at the meetings increased and the number of conversions grew, the more Satan tried to ensnare the new believers through vile and ferocious strategies. The bar owners no longer concealed their feelings, and threats of violence were made openly. Once during the week, Gray and his company of helpers were pelted with objects of every kind as they left the storefront chapel late at night. The police sent down a special force, and Virginia and Rachel were always under the protection of either Rollin or Dr. West. The influence of Rachel's singing had not diminished. In fact, each night seemed to bring with it a greater intensity and reality of the Spirit's presence.

Evangelist Gray at first questioned the prudence of holding a meeting on election night. But he had a simple rule of action and was always guided by it. The Spirit seemed to lead him to go ahead with the meeting, and so he went on as usual.

By the time the polls closed at six o'clock sharp, the people of Raymond had reached a fever of excitement. Never before had there been such a contest in their city. Never before had the godly and ungodly elements in the city been arrayed against each other in such an impressive fashion. It was unheard of for community leaders such as President Marsh of Lincoln College, Reverend Maxwell of First Church, the dean of the Cathedral, and so many other professional men and women to come into neighborhoods campaigning for good and attempting to stimulate the city's moral and Christian conscience. The politicians were astonished at the sight of these leaders; however, their astonishment did not curtail their activities. The fight grew hotter every hour, and when six o'clock came at last, neither side could have guessed the result with any certainty.

The meeting at the storefront chapel lasted until well after ten o'clock. It had been strange and remarkable. Reverend Maxwell had come down again at Gray's request. He was worn out by his day's activities, but the appeal from Gray came in such a way that he could not resist it. President Marsh was also present in the service. He had never been to the Rectangle district, and his curiosity was piqued as he heard of the evangelist's influence in that notorious part of the inner city. Dr. West and Rollin had come with Rachel and Virginia. Loreen, who was still staying with Virginia, sat near the piano. Throughout the service, her head was bowed, and she wept intermittently. When Rachel sang a song about wandering sheep, her weeping escalated to sobs. She knew the truth of Rachel's song.

The chapel was crowded. As on other occasions, there were disturbances outside throughout the service, and these interruptions increased as the night wore on. Gray decided it was not wise to prolong the service.

As the election returns began to come in, the streets and sidewalks in the Rectangle district became clogged with people who emerged from the bars after watching the results on television. They responded with jeers or cheers to every televised exit poll that was announced.

In spite of these distractions, Rachel's singing kept the crowd in the makeshift chapel from dissolving. There were a dozen or more conversions that night. Finally the people became restless and Gray closed the service, remaining a while with the converts for prayer and instruction.

Rachel, Virginia, Loreen, Rollin, President Marsh, Reverend Maxwell, and Dr. West left together, anxious to listen to the election results on their car radios. However, as they emerged from the building, they became aware that the streets of the Rectangle district were trembling and on the verge of a riot. As they pushed through the mobs in the narrow street on their way to their cars, they suddenly realized that their presence had garnered some unwelcome attention.

"There he is—the guy in the hat! He's the leader!" shouted a rough voice. President Marsh,

with his erect, commanding figure, was conspicuous in the group.

"How is the election going? It's too early to
know the result yet, isn't it?" He asked the question
aloud to the men milling around.

"We're hearing that the second and third wards
have gone solidly against the liquor interests. If
that's so, the booze boys won't be happy."

"Thank God! I hope it's true!" exclaimed
Maxwell. Then he turned to President Marsh, "I
think we are in danger here. We ought to get the
women to the cars," he urged.

"That's true," Marsh returned gravely. At that
very moment, a shower of stones and other
objects whizzed past them, and they realized that
the narrow street and sidewalk in front of the
storefront was now completely blocked by angry,
shouting men and women.

"Let's cut through here," Reverend Maxwell
called to the others. Marsh, Rollin Page, and Dr.
West placed the women between them and headed
down an alley into the darkness with the rowdy
mob following close behind. The angry people who
crowded into the Rectangle district that night saw
Marsh and Maxwell in particular as leaders in the

effort to rob them of their favorite haunts and, for some, their livelihoods as well.

As the small band of believers moved quickly down the alley, they were battered by a constant shower of mud and stones. Rachel later remembered that Rollin had jumped directly in front of her and in so doing had received several blows to his head and chest that might otherwise have seriously injured her.

The group was encouraged by the wail of police sirens, but before they could be rescued, a terrible thing happened. Loreen, terrified by their predicament, darted forward in front of Virginia and pushed her aside. At the same time, she looked up at the side of the building and screamed. Her action was so sudden that no one had time to see the face of the person who leaned out of an upstairs window and took aim at the group. A split second later, a crack of gunfire pierced the night and Loreen fell to the ground at their feet. Virginia screamed and threw her body over her friend. It was only a moment before a group of police officers reached the group and their fallen comrade.

President Marsh raised his arm and shouted over the howl that continued to rise from the wild mob.

"Stop!" he screamed, "You've killed someone!" The announcement served to sober the crowd only slightly.

"Is it true?" Maxwell asked as Dr. West knelt by Loreen's side, and Virginia supported her head.

"No, she's not dead, but her wound is severe, and I can't be sure she'll make it," Dr. West advised.

Loreen opened her eyes and smiled at Virginia, who wiped the blood from her face and gently bent over to kiss her forehead. Loreen smiled again, and the next minute her soul was in paradise.

The Rectangle district had stamped its image on Loreen, but she died a "new creature in Christ." Perhaps only Judgment Day will reveal the identity of her killer.

CHAPTER 15

Whoever follows me will never
walk in darkness.
John 8:12

Sunday morning dawned with a clear blue sky and a breath of spring air. Loreen's body lay in state at the mortuary where all Page family members were prepared for burial, and it seemed that the entire city had heard about the events of the night before. The disturbing news produced many conversations about the recent events that had so strangely affected the citizens of Raymond.

At First Church, Reverend Maxwell spoke to an unusually large congregation with a passion and a power that sprang directly from the profound experiences of the past few days. His people felt something of the old feeling of pride they once had enjoyed in his dramatic presentations. Only this was different. His words seemed to flow from a deep inner conviction and carried a note of sadness and rebuke.

Sad to say, the citizens of Raymond had gone to bed on election night only after hearing the television anchors declare that the offensive against the alcohol, tobacco, and gambling interests had been unsuccessful. The rumors in the Rectangle district had been in error. It was true that the victory was won by a very meager margin, but the results were the same. Raymond had voted to passify the city's corrupt administration for another year. Raymond stood condemned by the complacency of many professing Christians who failed to go to the polls, and many more who had chosen to vote with the status quo. Alcohol, drugs, gambling, and prostitution had won again. While no one admitted to wanting these elements in the city (except perhaps alcohol), the citizenry had once again elected men and women who would turn a blind eye to these destructive forces. What would Jesus do?

And this woman who had been brutally struck down by a coward's bullet—what about her? Were the consequences anything less than the logical sequence of the whole horrible system of rampant ungodliness? And in their silence, had not a portion of Raymond's Christians voted to support and perhaps doom a hundred Loreens?

With a trembling voice, Reverend Maxwell revealed the force of his disappointment to this

Sunday morning congregation. Men and women wept as he spoke. President Marsh sat quietly, his usual impressive bearing gone, and his head bowed as great tears rolled down his cheeks. He seemed unmindful of the fact that he was in a public worship service.

Edward Norman sat nearby. He seemed composed, but his lip trembled and he clutched at the end of the pew, feeling the emotion of truth as Reverend Maxwell spoke it. No man had given or suffered more to influence public opinion that week than Norman. The knowledge that their Christian conscience may have been aroused too late or too feebly, lay like a heavy weight of accusation upon the newspaper publisher's heart. What if he had begun to do as Jesus would do long ago? Who could tell what might have been accomplished by this time?

Seated in the choir, Rachel Winslow sat with her face bowed in her hands. When Reverend Maxwell concluded his message, she tried to sing the closing number, but her voice broke, and she could not finish.

All over the church, in the silence that followed the close of the sermon, one could hear the sound of sobs and weeping. When had First

Church yielded to such a baptism of tears? What had become of its traditionally unemotional order of worship? The answer is that these people had been challenged at the point of their deepest convictions. They had been living so long with their surface feelings that they had almost forgotten the deeper wells of life. Now that those deep emotions had reached the surface, the people were being convicted of the true meaning of discipleship.

Maxwell did not ask for volunteers to join those who had already pledged to do as Jesus would. But when the congregation was finally gone, he entered the side chapel to find that the original company of followers had greatly increased. The meeting after the service was moving. It glowed with the Spirit's presence and came alive with strong and lasting resolve to continue the war against evil in Raymond until its reign was broken forever. Since the first Sunday when the first group of volunteers had pledged themselves to do as Jesus would do, each of these meetings had been characterized by different impressions of the Holy Spirit. Today, the entire force of the gathering was directed toward this one great purpose. It was a meeting filled with prayers of contrition and confession; of strong yearning for a new and better city; and a general cry for deliverance from the vile influences that had taken residence in their midst.

If the First Church was deeply stirred by the events of the last week, the residents of the Rectangle district also felt strangely moved in its own way. The death of Loreen was not in itself so remarkable a fact, drive-by shootings had become rather common in Raymond; but it was her recent involvement with the people who strove for change that lifted her into special prominence and surrounded her death with more than ordinary importance. Everyone in the Rectangle district knew that Loreen was at this moment lying in her coffin in a mortuary up on the avenue. Exaggerated reports of the magnificence of the casket had already furnished material for eager gossip. They were eager to know the details of the funeral. Would it be public? What did Virginia Page intend to do? The Rectangle district had never before mingled even in this distant manner with the aristocracy of Raymond's privileged class. Evangelist Gray and his wife were besieged by inquirers who wanted to know what Loreen's friends and acquaintances could do to pay their last respects. Many of the recent converts had become her friends.

Loreen's funeral was set for Monday afternoon in the storefront chapel. Attendance for the event was so immense that the audience choked the chapel and overflowed out onto the sidewalk and into the street.

Gray sought Virginia and Reverend Maxwell and asked for their advice concerning the service. "I've always been opposed to large public funerals," said Gray, whose wholesome simplicity was one of his great sources of strength; "but the cry of these poor people who knew Loreen is so sincere that I do not know how to refuse their desire to see her and pay her some last honor. What do you think, Reverend Maxwell? I will be guided by your judgment in the matter. I am sure that whatever you and Virginia think best, will be right."

"I feel as you do," replied Maxwell. "I too have always had a great distaste for what seems like unnecessary drama at such times. But this seems different. The people of the Rectangle district will not come to First Church for the service. I think the most Christian thing will be to have the service at the chapel. What do you think, Virginia?"

"By all means, at the chapel," agreed Virginia. "Let her friends say good-bye to her in the surroundings she knew best." With only minor difficulty, arrangements for the funeral were finalized. This was the venue for one of the strangest happenings in the lives of all who attended the rites.

As it happened, on the afternoon of the funeral, a noted newspaper correspondent was passing through Raymond on his way to a convention in a neighboring city. He had heard about the contemplated service at the chapel and decided to attend. His description of the event was written in a graphic style that caught the attention of readers all over the nation on the day following the funeral:

> A unique and unusual funeral service was conducted Monday in Raymond. It was held in a storefront chapel on the wrong side of the tracks in a part of town known as the Rectangle district. Officiating was a traveling evangelist by the name of Reverend John Gray. The occasion was precipitated by the murder of a woman during an election night riot. It seems she had been recently converted during the evangelist's meetings, and was shot

while leaving in company with other converts and some of her friends.

By all accounts, she had been a homeless alcoholic, and yet the service in the chapel was as impressive as any I have witnessed in any metropolitan church for its most distinguished citizens.

In the first place, a most impressive choir sang. It astonished me to hear voices like those usually heard only in great churches or on the concert stage. But the most remarkable part of the music was a solo sung by a strikingly beautiful young woman, Miss Rachel Winslow who, if I remember correctly, has been much sought after by The National Opera Company, and who for some reason refused to accept a contract. She sang with great feeling and tears began to flow before she had finished a dozen words, which, of course, is not so strange at a funeral service. It's just that the voice itself was one in a thousand. I understand Rachel Winslow is a member of the First Church of Raymond choir and could probably command almost any amount of money as a professional singer. I guarantee she will be heard from soon.

Aside from the musical performances, the service itself was unusual. The officiant was an evangelist, a man of apparently very simple, unassuming style. He spoke a few words and then relinquished his pulpit to the Reverend Henry Maxwell, pastor of Raymond First Church. Reverend Maxwell spoke of the fact that the dead woman had been fully prepared to meet her Savior, but he also spoke of the tragic effects of alcohol, drugs, and gambling on the lives of other men and women like Loreen. I caught from the minister's remarks that he had only recently felt compelled to speak out against Raymond's unsavory elements. He certainly offered a very striking address, and yet it seemed in no way inappropriate for a funeral.

Then followed what was perhaps the strangest part of this service. The women in the chapel, at least a large part of them up near the coffin, began to softly sing a simple song that begins, "I was a wandering sheep." While the singing was going on, one row of women stood up and walked slowly past the casket, each one placing a flower upon it. When they sat down, another row filed past, leaving their flowers, all the time singing of a wandering sheep. The music was sung softly like falling rain when the wind is blowing gently. It was one of the simplest, and at the same time, one of the most impressive services I've ever attended. The three entrances to the storefront chapel were wide open and hundreds of people who could not get in, stood in the doorways, along the sidewalk, and spilled out into the street. All were as still as death itself, with an unusual sadness and solemnity for such rough-looking people. There must have been a hundred or more women, and I was told that many had only recently been converted at the meetings. I cannot describe the effect of that singing. Not a man sang a note. All women's voices, and they were so soft, and yet so distinct, that the effect was startling.

The service closed with another solo by Rachel Winslow, who sang, "The Ninety and Nine." Following Miss Winslow, the evangelist asked the congregation to bow their heads while he prayed. In order to make my departure time, I was forced to leave during the prayer. The last view I caught of the service as I drove away through the Rectangle district and past the great crowd pouring from the chapel, was that of the coffin being carried out by six of the women.

If Loreen's funeral impressed a passing stranger, it is not difficult to imagine the profound effect it had on those who had been so intimately connected with her life and death. Nothing had ever entered the Rectangle district that had moved it so deeply as Loreen's body in that coffin. And the Holy Spirit seemed to bless with special power the senseless death of this homeless child. For that night, He swept more than fifty souls, mostly women, into the fold of the Good Shepherd.

Reverend Maxwell's statements concerning the bar from whose window Loreen had been murdered, proved nearly true. The establishment was formally closed Monday, and Tuesday the authorities arrested the proprietors and charged them with the murder. But nothing could be proved against anyone, and before the end of the week, the bar was operating as usual.

CHAPTER 16

No one in Raymond, including the homeless of the Rectangle district, felt Loreen's death more keenly than Virginia. It came as a distinct personal loss for her. During the short week the woman had been sheltered in her home, Virginia's heart had been opened to a whole new vision for life. This vision was the topic of conversation as she met with Rachel the day after the funeral.

"I have got to do something with my money to help women like Loreen find a better way of life," Virginia said thinking of the women who assisted at the funeral. "I believe I have put together a good plan. I've discussed it with Rollin, and he seems interested in devoting a part of his money to a similar endeavor."

"How much do you have for the cause, Virginia?" asked Rachel. There was a time when she'd never have thought of asking such a personal question, but now it seemed as natural to talk frankly about money as about anything else that belonged to God.

"I have about $2 million available. Maybe more. Rollin has at least that much, although he now bitterly regrets his previous bent toward extravagance—B.C."

"B.C.?" asked Rachel.

"Before conversion. We're both eager to make all the reparations we can. 'What would Jesus do with this money?' We want to answer that question honestly and wisely. I'm confident that the money I've committed to invest in the *Daily News* is in line with Christ's probable action. With Raymond's severe social ills, it is as necessary that we have a daily paper that espouses Christian values, as it is to have a church or a college. So I am satisfied that Mr. Norman will know how to use the $2 million I have committed to invest—to the glory of God and the salvation of Raymond.

"About my other plan, Rachel, Rollin and I want you to work with us. We intend to purchase a large portion in the Rectangle district. The square block with the storefront chapel has been in litigation for years. We plan to secure the entire tract as soon as the courts have settled the title. For some time, I have been studying the possibility of investing in inner-city residential projects. I'm not ready to say what would be best for Raymond, but I do know that my money— rather God's—can build decent, low-income housing for homeless and struggling women like Loreen. I plan to be more than a do-gooder dispensing money. God help me! I want to be completely involved—body, mind, and spirit."

Rachel's eyes sparked, "But what good will housing do if the conditions that destroy women like Loreen continue to be present in Raymond?"

"You're right, Rachel. Our money and labors are for nothing as long as City Hall allows these purveyors of vice and corruption to thrive."

Suddenly Virginia stood and began to pace the hall. Rachel watched her for a moment, and then spoke.

"From my rather limited perspective, I believe you're right. But, Virginia, you can't overlook the good that will be done with this money—City Hall or no City Hall. Sooner or later the Christian forces in our city will triumph."

Virginia paused near Rachel, and her eyes had a new light.

"I believe that too, Rachel. The number of believers who are eager to do as Jesus would is increasing. But now, dear friend, I want us to consider your part in this plan for reforming the Rectangle district. Your voice is a powerful force for good. Why don't you consider organizing some sort of music school for inner city young people? You could give them the benefit of your training."

"Oh, Virginia, I don't know. . . . "

"Have you ever heard such inspiring, untrained voices as those we heard at the funeral yesterday? Rachel, what an opportunity! I'll see to it that you have all you need to run such a program."

Before Virginia finished, Rachel was convinced. This new idea gripped her heart and mind like nothing else had. And it seemed to be a useful and pleasing way to use her talent.

"I'm convinced, Virginia—absolutely convinced. So that I should gladly give my life to the kind of service you've suggested. I believe that's exactly what Jesus wants me to do."

"What a combination—your talents and personal enthusiasm . . . ," Virginia began, but stopped when Rollin walked into the library.

He hesitated a moment, and then seeing the women talking, he turned to politely slip out. But Virginia called after him.

Rollin sat down, acknowledging Rachel with a nod. Then the three of them discussed their future plans. Apparently Rollin was comfortable talking about his plans in front of Rachel, though his usual outgoing personality was unmistakenly shy in her presence. The past difficulties between them seemed to have been entirely forgotten in deference to his new life and priorities. When Rollin was called to the phone, Rachel and Virginia began to talk of other things.

"By the way, what has become of Jasper Chase?" Virginia asked innocently. Rachel flushed, so Virginia added with a smile, "I suppose he is writing another book. Is he going to put you into this one, Rachel? You know, I always suspected that our Mr. Chase had done that very thing in his first novel."

"Virginia," Rachel spoke with the frankness that had always existed between the two friends, "Jasper Chase almost proposed to me the other night. He would have, if —" Rachel stopped and sat with her hands clasped in her lap.

"Virginia, not so long ago I thought I loved him as he said he loved me. But when he spoke, I felt like an icy hand was gripping my heart, so I said what I knew I had to say. I told him no and I have not seen him since. That was the night of the first conversions at the storefront chapel."

"I'm glad for you," said Virginia quietly.

"Why?" asked Rachel a little startled.

"Because, I've never really liked Jasper Chase. He's too cold and calculating. I don't like to judge but I've always mistrusted his sincerity—even when he took the pledge at the church with the rest of us."

Rachel looked thoughtfully at Virginia.

"I have never given my heart to him, but he did touch my emotions, and I admire his skill as a writer. I have thought at times that I cared a good deal for him. I think perhaps if he had spoken to me at any other time than the one he chose, I could easily have persuaded myself that I loved him. But not now."

Again Rachel paused suddenly, and when she looked up at Virginia again there were tears on her face. Virginia came to her and put her arm around her shoulders.

After Rachel's departure, Virginia sat in the library thinking about the conversation she had had with her friend and marveling at the confidence Rachel had just shown in her plans. Just the same, Virginia felt certain that there had been more on Rachel's mind than she was willing to confide at that time.

As Virginia left the library, she saw Rollin and the two walked up and down the long hall arm in arm, as they had lately been in the habit of doing. It was easy for their conversation to center on Rachel because of the role she was to play in the plans for the Rectangle property.

"Have you ever known anyone nearly as gifted as Rachel who was so willing to give her life to help others? She plans to give music lessons in the city, depending on the proceeds to make a living, and then she will also be providing lessons for the residents of the Rectangle district free of charge. I do so admire and respect her commitment to give the benefit of her training and her voice to those who can least afford it."

"It's certainly a good example of self-sacrifice," replied Rollin stiffly.

Virginia looked at him questioningly, "But don't you think it's an unusual example? Can you imagine—," here Virginia named half a dozen famous opera singers—"doing anything like this?"

"No, I can't," Rollin answered. "Neither can I imagine any of your friends doing what *you* are doing, Virginia."

"Any more than I can imagine any of *your* friends doing what you're doing, Rollin." The two walked on in silence for the length of the hall.

"Getting back to Rachel," began Virginia again, "why are you so distant with her? I don't think she understands. Perhaps you could try to be warmer."

Obviously agitated, Rollin stopped walking. Taking his arm from Virginia's, he walked alone to the end of the hall, then returned to her. He stood looking at the floor with his hands behind his back, then looked up sharply and asked, "Virginia, haven't you learned my secret?"

Virginia looked bewildered, then her face flushed, a lifetime indication that she understood.

"I've never loved anyone but Rachel Winslow," Rollin spoke calmly enough now. "That day she was here when you talked about her refusal to join the concert company, I asked her to be my wife. She refused me, as I knew she would. And she gave as her reason the fact I had no purpose in life, which was true enough. Now that I have found a purpose and am a new man, it seems impossible for me to say anything. I owe my salvation to the ministry of God through Rachel's singing. That night in the storefront chapel, I can honestly say that I never thought of her voice as anything except God's message to me. I believe that my romantic love for Rachel was for the time merged into my personal love for God." Rollin stood silently for a moment, and then went on with more emotion. "I still love her, Virginia, but I don't think she will ever love me." He stopped and looked earnestly into his sister's face.

"I don't know about that," Virginia answered. She noted Rollin's handsome face, his marks of dissipation nearly gone. There was no question, her brother was now a man. Why shouldn't Rachel come to love him in time? Surely the two were well-suited for each other, especially now that their purposes in life were motivated by their faith in Christ.

Virginia related her thoughts to Rollin, but it didn't give him much comfort. When the conversation closed, Virginia had the impression that Rollin meant to go his own way with his personal evangelism project for men, and while he would not avoid Rachel, neither would he look for occasions to see her. Rollin did not fully trust his ability to control his feelings, and he dreaded the possibility of a second refusal.

CHAPTER 17

Early the next day Virginia went down to the *Daily News* office to see Edward Norman and arrange the details of her part in the financial matters of the paper. Reverend Maxwell was present for the conference, and the three agreed that whatever Jesus would do in regard to the daily details of running the paper, would serve as a mandate for their own decisions.

"Let me show you my 'battle plan,'" Edward Norman joked. "I have written out some of the things that I believe Jesus would do if He were walking in my shoes." Norman read from a yellow legal pad, reminding Pastor Maxwell of his own effort to conceptualize Jesus' probable action. Milton Wright attempted the same exercise in his business. "I have headed this document, 'What would Jesus do as Edward Norman, CEO of Norman Communications and publisher of Raymond's daily newspaper?'"

1. Jesus would never allow a sentence or a graphic in his paper that could be construed in any way as being untrue, crude, or sensational.

2. Jesus would probably institute a political editorial policy of non-partisan patriotism, always looking upon all political questions in the light of their relationship to the Kingdom of God. He would advocate measures consistent with the welfare of the people, always on the basis of "What is right?" never on the basis of "What is in the best interests of this or that party?"

Edward Norman looked up from the paper. "You understand that is my opinion of Jesus' probable action on political matters in a daily paper. I am not passing judgment on other newspaper people who may have a different conception of Jesus' probable action than mine. I am simply trying to answer honestly, 'What would Jesus do as Edward Norman?' And the answer I find is what I have written here."

3. The bottom line of any paper overseen by Jesus would be to seek and do His Father's will. That is, His main purpose in publishing a newspaper would be to relate world and local events to the larger cause—God's will and purposes. His first concern would not be financial or

political, but would be to so conduct His paper that it would be evident to all His subscribers that He was trying to seek first the Kingdom of God.

4. All untrue and questionable advertising would be refused, regardless of income.

5. Jesus' relationship with His employees would reflect his loving concern for body, mind, and spirit.

"Perhaps you can tell at this point," explained Norman, again looking up, "that I'm of the opinion that Jesus would employ some form of revenue sharing. I'm working out such a plan right now, and I'm confident it will be successful. I believe a Christian employer must introduce the personal concerns for employees into his or her business. And, as I have already said, that concern would be expressed not only in personal interest but in a sharing of the business profits."

6. As publisher of a daily paper today, Jesus would give maximum advantage to the work of the Christian world. He would devote as much space as possible to editorializing about the need for reform

of sociological problems, of para-church work and similar movements.

7. Jesus would do all in His power to fight against the interests of alcohol, tobacco, drugs, gambling, and prostitution as enemies of the human race. This would be His conviction regardless of public sentiment and His subscription list.

Again Edward Norman looked up and removed his glasses. "I state my honest conviction on this point. Of course, I do not pass judgment on the Christian men and women who are producing other types of newspapers today. But as I interpret Jesus, I believe He would use His paper's influence to remove these vices entirely from the political and social life of the nation."

8. I'm convinced that Jesus would not issue a Sunday edition if it meant filling homes with unwholesome features and news stories.

9. Jesus would print the news of the world that people ought to know. Among the things they do not need to know, and which would not be published, include the detailed accounts of lurid crime, conjecture

about public figures, scandals in private families, or any other human events which in any way would conflict with the first point mentioned in this outline.

10. Jesus would use the investment that has been committed to us, in order to secure the best and strongest writers who are able to write from a Christian perspective. Their personal lives will have to be as sterling as their writing ability.

Edward Norman finished reading his plan.

"This is no more than a vague outline. I have a hundred ideas for making the paper powerful that I have not yet thought through. What I've just read to you should be thought of as a first draft. I have discussed my feelings with other newspaper publishers and editors. Some of them say I will have a weak, 'churchy' propaganda sheet. One told me I will become the next famous televangelist! Why do you suppose when people want to characterize something as particularly feeble, they call it 'churchy'? Those people ought to know that the church is one of the strongest, most powerful influences in this country today. Be assured, this paper will not be weak because it is good. My only overriding concern is this—will the Christian people of Raymond support my paper? There are more than 600,000 church members in this city. If half of them will stand by the *Daily News*, the life of this paper will be assured. What do you think, Pastor Maxwell, is this kind of support a possibility?"

"I don't know enough about your profession to give an intelligent answer, but I do believe in the paper with all my heart. If it lives a year, as Virginia said, I believe there is no limit to what can be done. It seems to me that your assignment is to issue a 'daily' that contains the Christian elements of strength, intelligence, and common sense, while avoiding bigotry, fanaticism, narrow-mindedness, and anything else contrary to the Spirit of Jesus. Such a paper will call for the best that human thought and action can give. The greatest minds in the world would tax their abilities trying to produce such a paper."

Edward Norman spoke humbly. "I'm sure I'll make a great many mistakes. I'll need a great deal of wisdom. But I want to do as Jesus would. 'What would He do?' I have asked it and will continue to ask it. I'm ready to live with the results."

Virginia's eyes sparkled. "I think all of us are beginning to understand the meaning of the command to 'grow in the grace and knowledge of our Lord and Savior Jesus Christ.'"

"That's true," replied Pastor Maxwell. "I am beginning to understand that I cannot interpret the probable action of Jesus until I know more about His Spirit. The greatest question in all of human life is, 'What would Jesus do?' I believe the answer can only be found as we grow in the knowledge of Jesus Himself. We must know Jesus before we can imitate Him."

When Virginia and Edward Norman had finalized the arrangements, the publisher had received a check for $2 million to provide for the establishment of a daily newspaper espousing Christian values. After Virginia and Maxwell left, Norman closed the office door and dropped to his knees for some quality time alone with God. He was like a child asking for help from an all-powerful Father. As if in answer came the promise, *If any of you lacks wisdom, he should ask God, who gives generously to all without finding fault, and it will be given to him* (James 1:5). Surely his prayer would be answered.

Two months passed. For the newspaper and the praying group at First Church, they were a near blur of activity and wonderful results. In spite of the approaching summer heat, the disciples' after-church meetings continued with enthusiasm and power. Evangelist John Gray, feeling that his work was finished, discontinued the meetings at the storefront chapel, and to the casual observer passing through the Rectangle district, the area looked about the same as it always had. The real changes could only be seen in the hundreds of lives that had been touched by God. The bars were still operating and prostitutes continued to loiter on the street corners, along with druggies waiting for a dealer. Those rescued by the evangelist were quickly replaced by fresh victims. Satan recruited his ranks very quickly.

Henry Maxwell and Mary canceled their trip abroad. Instead, they used the money to quietly arrange for a summer Vacation Bible School for the children of the Rectangle district. The pastor and wife of First Church would never forget the month they spent planning and overseeing the event. First Church young people who had become part of the promise-making group staffed the school. The storefronts on either side of the chapel were pressed into service, along with a rubbish-strewn lot across the street, which was cleaned up and used as a play yard. Folding banquet tables and chairs from the church were used to outfit makeshift classrooms. In addition, curriculum, craft materials, refreshments, games, prizes, audio-visuals, and all the other physical elements of a well-planned and executed VBS were secured, many from donations made by downtown merchants.

"Mary," Maxwell addressed his wife one afternoon during the recreation period, "if we are ever going to make an impact on the Rectangle district, we will have to do it through the children. Our services with Gray really did not affect them, except those whose parents were touched."

Mary smiled, "Henry, I've been praying that God will use this Vacation Bible School for that very reason. This has been my 'What would Jesus do?' project. That's why I suggested scuttling the European trip." Mary patted her husband's hand, "We will win many children through this summer project. I see it as an investment in eternal things."

Maxwell replied to several church-member inquiries, "I don't feel Mary and I need a vacation this summer. God has given me assurance that He's caring for us."

Throughout the summer months, Reverend Maxwell grew in his knowledge of the Lord. First

Church was still in the Spirit's grip. The Vacation Bible School came to an end with requests that a regular Sunday school be established in the Rectangle district. "We'll have to pray about that," was Maxwell's response.

Other factors were at work in First Church. There were many among the membership who had not joined the disciple group. These folks regarded the movement as a fanatical interpretation of Christian duty. They were "praying" for a return to the old familiar ways. Meanwhile, the disciples continued to be under the influence of the Holy Spirit, freeing their pastor for ministry in the community, which he dispatched with great joy, including the noon meetings at the steel mill, as he had promised Alexander Powers he would.

Early one afternoon in August, after a day of unusual coolness, Jasper Chase walked to his office window and looked out. On his desk lay a manuscript. As always, Rachel Winslow was in his thoughts, though he had not seen or spoken to her since that evening when he had determined to declare his feelings. Jasper's sensitivity to what occurred with Rachel had thrust him into an isolation intensified by his sequestered habits as an author.

All through the heat of summer, he had been writing. The book was nearly finished. In reaction to Rachel's dismissal, he had thrown himself into writing with feverish commitment. He had not forgotten his pledge of discipleship made with the other members of First Church. He found himself asking over and over again, "In my circumstance, what would Jesus do? Would He write this story?" The novel was a light, satirical novel. It had no purpose except to amuse. Its moral teaching was not negative, but neither was it strongly Christian. Jasper Chase knew that such a story would probably sell. He knew the character types he created would be well received, and he also knew that there would be many who would devote themselves to uncovering each character's true identity. *What would Jesus do?* he wondered. *For starters*, he said to himself, *Jesus would never write such a book.* The question intruded on him at the most inopportune times and deeply disturbed him. The standard of Jesus was too ideal for an author. Of course, Jesus would use His powers to produce something useful or helpful or with a purpose. So, why was he, Jasper Chase, writing this novel? The answer was obvious. They consisted of the two reasons every author writes—for money and fame. It was no secret that his particular motive touched one of those two reasons. He was already wealthy and therefore, had no great temptation to write for money. Instead, he was urged on by his desire for fame. He had to write this kind of material if he was to solidify his reputation as an important author. But, he couldn't help wondering, *What really would Jesus do?* The question plagued him even more than Rachel's refusal. *Was he going to break his pledge— his commitment? Had his pledge really meant that much after all?* he asked.

Still standing at the window, Jasper saw Rollin Page emerge from a restaurant across the street. He couldn't help noticing that the young man had an unusually light step as he walked down the sidewalk to his car. He looked like a man with purpose, and he carried a book of some kind. *Probably a Bible,* Jasper thought.

Returning to his desk, he turned over some papers, then returned to the window. Rollin was still on the street, but now he was talking with Rachel Winslow. She must have been meeting Virginia for lunch. Jasper continued to watch as the two walked to Rollin's car, which was parked at the curb. Rollin opened the passenger door for Rachel, and then went around to the driver's side.

Jasper watched the car disappear in the traffic, then he turned back to his word processor and began to write. By the time he had finished a draft of the last page in the last chapter, it was nearly dark outside his window and in the room. "What would Jesus do?" He had finally answered the question by turning his back on his Lord. The darkness began to enshroud him. He had deliberately chosen his course, urged on by his disappointment and loss.

Jesus replied, No one who puts his hand to the plow and looks back is fit for service in the kingdom of God (Luke 9:62).

CHAPTER 18

What is that to you? You must follow me.
John 21:22

When Rollin left the restaurant after a conversation about Christ with two of his old friends, and started to his car, he was not thinking about Rachel Winslow and did not expect to see her. But there she stood on the opposite side of the street from where his car was parked. It would be less than truthful not to admit that the sight of her made him catch his breath. Crossing the street, he attempted to be nonchalant about seeing her, but he was sure that his smile and quickened step gave him away.

"I've just had lunch with Virginia," explained Rachel. "She tells me the arrangements are almost complete for the transfer of the Rectangle property."

"Finally. It has been a tedious case in the courts. Did Virginia show you the plans and specs for the building?"

"We looked over a good many. It's astonishing how many ideas Virginia has managed to come up with for this project. She's amazing."

"Virginia has learned more about the possibilities for inner city ministries than a good many professionals. She's spent nearly all summer gathering information."

"Can I give you a lift home?" asked Rollin. When she agreed, he found himself beginning to feel more at ease. He smiled shyly as he opened the car door for her. *This topic is safe,* he thought. *We're on common ground.*

As the car pulled away from the curb, Rachel asked, "What have you been doing all summer? I haven't seen much of you." She quickly looked down as she felt her face flush. *I wonder if I'm showing too much interest?* she thought.

"I've been pretty busy," Rollin replied.

Rachel persisted. "Tell me something about what you're doing. You say so little. Have I a right to ask?" Rachel was surprised by her own frankness. Nevertheless, she turned to Rollin for an answer.

"Yes, certainly," he replied with an encouraging smile. "I am not so certain that I can tell you much. I have been spending time with my old friends and trying to find ways to tell them about life in Christ."

He stopped suddenly as if he were almost afraid to go on. Rachel did not venture to suggest anything.

"For the past few months, I've been a member of the same First Church disciple group to which you and Virginia belong," continued Rollin. "I've made the same pledge—to do as I believe Jesus would do—and I've been trying to live my life and conduct my affairs accordingly."

"That's what I find difficult to understand. Virginia told me about your pledge, and it's wonderful to know that you have made the same commitment we have made. But, I wonder how wise it is to spend so much time with your old friends?"

"You've asked me a rather direct question, so let me take a stab at a direct answer," Rollin replied, smiling again. By this time, they were parked in Rachel's driveway.

"After that night in the chapel, I asked myself how I could redeem my life. I had to satisfy my need for Christian discipleship. The more I thought about it, the more I was driven to a place where I knew, in the words of Reverend Maxwell, I must take up the cross. Did you ever think that there are 'up and outers' as well as 'down and outers'? Churches and the government look after the poor. Churches send money and missionaries to the lost overseas, but most give no thought to the affluent young people in this city. No one reaches out to them, and yet no group of people need to know the love of Christ more than these well-fixed souls. I finally admitted that I needed to be a missionary to my kind. I know them and understand the way they think. God has not asked me to reach out to the residents of the Rectangle district. But, I think I could reach some of the young, affluent types who have too much money and too much time on their hands. So, that's what I've been trying to do. It's what Jesus wants me to do. This is my cross."

Rollin lowered his voice to the point that Rachel had difficulty hearing him. She wanted to ask what his witnessing methods were, but didn't dare, wishing not to offend him in any way. Her interest in his plan was larger than mere curiosity. Rollin Page was no longer the egocentric young man who had asked her to be his wife. She could not help but think of him as an entirely new person.

Sitting in Rachel's driveway reminded Rollin that this was the very spot where he had asked Rachel why she could not love him. Rachel must have remembered, too. They were both stricken with a sudden shyness. Rachel had not forgotten that day and Rollin could not. She finally broke a long silence by asking what she had not found words to say before.

"When you witness to your old friends, what sort of reception do they give you? What do you say to them?"

Rollin was relieved when Rachel spoke. He answered quickly.

"Oh, it depends on the person. A good many of them already think I'm nuts, so I try to be wise and not provoke any unnecessary criticism. But you would be surprised to know how many of my friends have responded to my words. Only a few nights ago, I was able to engage almost a dozen men in a conversation about religion. The best thing, though, is that I have had the great joy of seeing some of my old friends accept Christ, give up certain destructive habits, and begin new lives in the same way I have. 'What would Jesus do?' I keep asking it."

"How do these people respond to you, Rollin?"

"Happily, I've found that my friends are not shy with me, and I think that is a good sign. Another thing is that some of them have actually shown an interest in helping out in the Rectangle district when it is started up. I believe they could make a powerful difference."

Rollin's face glowed with enthusiasm about the subject, which had now become a part of his real life. Rachel realized that Rollin bore a deep, underlying seriousness which characterizes a crossbearer, even though he seemed to carry it with such joy.

Rachel asked, "Do you remember that I once accused you of living without a sense of purpose?" Rollin looked into Rachel's eyes, as she continued, "I have to say something to you, Rollin. I see in you a 'new creature.' I honor you for your courage and your obedience to the promise you have made. The life you are living is a noble one."

Rollin trembled inside. His agitation was more than he could control. Rachel could not help but see it. They sat in silence, until Rollin said at last, "Thank you, Rachel. It's been worth more than I can tell you to hear those words." He looked steadily into her eyes for only a moment, but in that moment, Rachel was able to read his love for her.

Rachel went into the house and to her room, where she sat at a dressing table with her face in her hands. Looking at herself in the mirror she confessed, "I believe I know what it means to be loved by a good man. I love Rollin Page."

Rachel stood and walked to the dormer window and watched the traffic in the street below. She was deeply moved, not because of regret or sorrow, but because a new joy had come over her. If anyone had seen Rachel dancing around her room in happy abandonment, they would have had no doubt that this beautiful young woman was in love. She had entered another circle of experience. Later in the day, she rejoiced with great gladness that her Christian discipleship allowed her to experience the feeling of human love so beautifully based in divine love.

As Rollin left Rachel's driveway, he found himself holding tenaciously to a treasured hope that had eluded him since Rachel rejected his vow of love. It was in that hope, he went on with his work as the days sped on. His success as a witness for Christ seemed to increase following his most recent conversation with Rachel. To paraphrase the hymn writer, he seemed to have a "deep, settled peace."

The last summer month was removed from calendars and Raymond was once more facing the rigor of her winter season. Virginia had been able to accomplish a part of her plan for "capturing the

Rectangle," as she called it. But the razing of old buildings and the construction of new, low-cost housing was an endeavor too great for completion that fall. Yet, a million dollars in the hands of a person who truly wants to do as Jesus would, ought to accomplish wonders for humanity in a short time. Reverend Maxwell walked over to the construction site one day after a noon hour with the steel mill staff, and found himself amazed to see how much had been accomplished.

Walking from the mill to his parked car, Maxwell decided to take an impromptu tour of the district. Again, he was made aware of how much easier his groups' jobs would be if there were no alcohol and drugs, not to mention gambling and prostitution. The minister was overwhelmed by the magnitude of the work left to be done. The tempter came close and whispered in his ear, "How much really has been done for the Rectangle district after all?" Even counting the contributions Virginia, Rachel, and Rollin were making as well as Reverend Gray's groundbreaking work at the chapel, where had it actually counted in any substantial way?

Fighting off a spirit of failure, Maxwell reminded himself that the redemptive work begun and carried on by the Holy Spirit with His displays of power at First Church and, of course, in the chapel meetings, had had a mighty and lasting effect on the lives of the citizens of Raymond. *After all, Rome wasn't built in a day,* he thought. Then he answered himself, *No, but Rome's fall came about because of the same vices that are attacking the citizens of Raymond.*

He walked past bars, gambling parlors, pimps, and drug dealers and saw as much brutality, squalor, open misery, and degradation as ever. The sight sickened him.

I wonder, he thought, *how much cleansing could be accomplished with a million dollars poured into this cesspool? Wasn't the source of so much human misery directly related to the drinking establishments and gambling halls? What could even such unselfish Christian discipleship as Virginia and Rachel's do to lessen the stream of vice and crime as long as it was approved by City Hall?* It appeared to him to be a practical waste of precious lives for these young women to throw themselves into this earthly hell, when for every soul rescued by their sacrifice, the forces of darkness made two more that needed rescuing.

He could not escape the obvious, and it was the same conclusion reached by Rachel and Virginia: nothing permanent would ever be done until the Rectangle district was rid of its crime-producing elements. Henry Maxwell went back to his car and worked through his afternoon with a firmer conviction to clean up City Hall and clear out the self-serving and destructive forces at work in Raymond.

If Reverend Maxwell felt alcohol and drugs were hard at work in the daily life of Raymond, no less was First Church and its committed company of disciples. Standing at the very center of the movement, it was often difficult to judge its power and effectiveness as someone from the outside might have done. But, Raymond itself felt the change in many ways and did not know the reasons for it.

Winter was almost over, and a bright new year gleamed on the horizon. Sunday was the one-year anniversary of what in many ways was the most remarkable day in First Church history—the day their minister and church members pledged to make no decision without first asking, "What would Jesus do." This anniversary day was probably more important than any of the First

Church disciples realized. The year had made history so fast and so seriously that most people in and out of the church were not yet able to grasp its significance. The day itself, which marked the completion of a year of discipleship, was characterized by testimonies, revelations, and confessions. There was an overwhelming spirit of God's presence, and those who participated were incapable of grasping the magnitude of their pledges—not in their own church but also across the country.

As it happened, the week before anniversary Sunday, the Reverend Calvin Bruce, doctor of Divinity of the Nazareth Avenue Church, Chicago, was in Raymond, where he had come to visit old friends, and see his seminary classmate, Henry Maxwell. Because he was a guest of the Maxwells, he attended First Church and was soon caught up in the excitement of what was happening. His account of the events in Raymond, and especially of that Sunday, may throw more light on the entire situation than any description or record from other sources.

CHAPTER 19

[Letter from Reverend Calvin Bruce, doctor of Divinity, of the Nazareth Avenue Church, Chicago, to Reverend Philip A. Caxton, doctor of Divinity, New York City.]

D*ear Philip:*

It is late Sunday night, but I am intensely awake and so overflowing with what I saw and heard this morning that I'm driven to write you an account of the situation in Raymond as I have perceived it, and also because it apparently came to a climax today. So this is my only excuse for writing so long a letter at this time.

I believe you remember Henry Maxwell from seminary days. The last time I visited you in New York, I believe you said that you had not seen him since we graduated. I remember Maxwell as a refined, scholarly man. When he was called to First Church of Raymond within a year after leaving the seminary, I said to my wife, "Raymond has made a good choice. Maxwell will serve them well."

Henry has been here in Raymond for eleven years, and I understand that until a year ago, he had gone along with the regular course of the ministry, drawing respect for himself from his parishioners. His was known to be the largest and wealthiest church in Raymond. All the best people attended regularly, and most belonged. The choir was famous for its music, especially for one of its sopranos, a Miss Rachel Winslow, of whom I shall have more to say.

On the whole, as I understand the facts, Maxwell was in a comfortable position with a good salary, pleasant surroundings, and a relaxed, refined, wealthy, respectable congregation—the kind of church almost any young man or woman in the seminary would look forward to and consider desirable.

But a year ago today, Maxwell came into his church on Sunday morning, and at the close of the service, made the astounding proposition that the members of his church volunteer for a year not to make any decision or take any course of action without first asking the question, "What would Jesus do?" and, after answering it, to do what in their honest judgment He would do, regardless of what the consequences might be to them.

The effect of this proposition, as it has been followed and obeyed by a group of his church members, has been so remarkable that, as you know, the attention of the whole country has been directed to the movement. I call it a "movement" because from the action taken today, it seems probable that what has been tried here will expand into the other churches and cause a revolution in Christian discipleship.

In the first place, Maxwell tells me he was astonished at the response of his congregation to his proposition. Some of the most prominent members in the church made the pledge to do as Jesus would. Among them were Edward Norman, CEO of Norman Communications, which includes newspapers and television stations. As publisher of the local Daily News, Norman has caused a sensation in the newspaper world. The list also includes Milton Wright, one of the leading merchants in Raymond, with stores and outlet malls around the state. Alexander Powers was the superintendent of production at Raymond Steel. His decision to hand over evidence of violations of the interstate commerce laws cost him his position and made quite a stir. Virginia Page, a member of one of Raymond's wealthiest families, has lately invested an enormous amount of money in the Edward Norman's Daily News in an effort to ensure that the newspaper is able to continue its policy of supporting reform and Christian values. She has also purchased property in the poorest part of Raymond, referred to as the Rectangle district, for the purpose of providing low-income housing for homeless and struggling women. Rachel Winslow, whose reputation as a singer is now well-known, has devoted her talent to volunteer work among the girls and women who make up a large part of the city's worst and most abandoned population.

In addition to these prominent Raymond citizens, there has been a gradually increasing number of concerned Christians not only from First Church but from other churches as well who have also pledged to do as Jesus would do. The majority of these individuals come from church youth movements. These young people say that they have already embodied in their personal commitments the same principle in the words, "I promise Him that I will strive to do whatever He would have me do."

I am sure the first question you will ask is, "What has been the result of this attempt? What has it accomplished or how has it changed the church and/or the community?"

The result of the pledge upon First Church has been twofold. It has brought about a spirit of

Christian fellowship, which Maxwell tells me never before existed and now impresses him as being very nearly what the Christian koinonia of the apostolic churches must have been like. As a result, it has divided the church into two distinct groups. Those who have not taken the pledge regard the others as foolishly literal in their attempt to imitate the example of Jesus. Some of them have come out of the church and no longer attend or have transferred their membership to another congregation. Some members have contributed to internal strife, and I heard rumors of an attempt on their part to force Maxwell's resignation. I do not know that this element is very strong in the church. It has been held in check by a wonderful continuance of spiritual power, which dates from a year ago when the pledge was first taken, and also by the fact that so many of the most prominent members have been identified with the movement.

The effect of all this on Maxwell is marked. I heard him preach in our State Association four years ago. He impressed me at the time as having considerable power in dramatic delivery and presence, of which he himself was somewhat aware. His sermon was well-written and abounded in what seminary students used to call "fine passages."

The effect of it was what an average congregation would call "pleasing." This morning, I heard Maxwell preach again, for the first time since then. He is not the same man. He gives me the impression of one who has passed through a crisis. He tells me this is simply a new definition of Christian discipleship. He certainly has changed many of his old habits and many of his old views. His attitude on the social ills of Raymond—especially the alcohol and tobacco lobbies— radically opposes the stance he held a year ago.

In his entire ministry, his preaching and parish work, I find he has made a complete change. So far as I can understand, the idea that is moving him now is that the Christianity of our times must represent a more literal imitation of Jesus, especially as concerning the suffering of others. Several times in the course of our conversation, he quoted to me verses from Peter: To this you were called, because Christ suffered for you, leaving you an example, that you should follow in his steps (1 Peter 2:21). He seems filled with the conviction that what the church needs today more than anything else is this idea of joyful suffering for Jesus. I do not know if I agree with him entirely, but, Philip, it is certainly astonishing to note *the results of this idea and how it has influenced this city and this church.*

You may wonder about the personal consequences these individuals have encountered since making this pledge and attempting to be true to it. Those consequences are, as I have said, a part of each person's history and cannot be told in detail. Some of them I can give you so that you may see that this form of discipleship is not merely sentiment or posturing for effect.

For instance, take the case of Mr. Powers, superintendent of production at Raymond Steel, whom I spoke about earlier. When he acted upon evidence which was incriminating to the company, through no fault of his own, he resigned his management post and returned to the job he held as a young man in the business, taking a drastic cut in wages. All of this has happened because Powers asked himself if Christ could be associated with such illegal activities.

By the way, Philip, I understand in this connection that the Commission, for one reason or another, has postponed action on this case, and it is rumored that the company will pass into a receivership very soon. The president of the mill, who according to the evidence submitted by Powers, was the principal offender, has resigned. I met Mr. Powers at the church yesterday. He impressed me as a man who had, like Maxwell, gone through a crisis in character. I could not help thinking of him as being good material for the church of the first century when the disciples had all things in common.

Or I could cite the case of Mr. Norman, owner and publisher of the Daily News. He risked his entire fortune in obedience to what he believed would have been Jesus' action and revolutionized his entire concept of the paper at the risk of failure. I enclose a copy of today's edition. I want you to read it carefully. To my mind, it is one of the most interesting and remarkable papers ever printed in the United States. It is open to criticism, but what could any mere man attempt in this line that would be free from at least some criticism. All in all, it is so far above the ordinary conception of a daily newspaper, that I am amazed at the result. He tells me that the paper is beginning to be read more and more by the city's Christian community. Norman appeared to be confident of the paper's final success. Read his editorial on the money questions, also the one on the coming election in Raymond when the question of the city's stance on legalizing gambling and easing of its liquor license requirements will *again be an issue. Both articles are logical and reflect clear thinking. Norman says he never begins an editorial or, in fact, any negotiation without first asking, "What would Jesus do?" The result is certainly apparent.*

Then there is Milton Wright, Raymond's most successful merchandiser. He has, I am told, so revolutionized his company that no man is more beloved today in Raymond. His own employees have an affection for him that is very touching. During the winter, while he was lying in a hospital room suffering from a serious illness, scores of employees volunteered to watch and help in any way possible, and his return to his company was greeted with a marked demonstration of appreciation. All this has been brought about by the recognition that his employees are the key to his success. Consequently, he has instituted a better health plan, revenue sharing, better working conditions, and a genuine sense of caring. This caring spirit is not mere words, but the company itself is carried on under a system of cooperation that is not patronizing.

Other merchandisers look upon Milton Wright as odd. It is a fact, however, that while his overhead has risen, his company has increased appreciatively.

Today Wright is respected and honored as one of the best and most successful men in Raymond.

And then there is Rachel Winslow. She has chosen to give her great talent to the underprivileged of the city. Her plans include a music school where classes in vocal music and a trained student choir shall be a feature. She is enthusiastic about her life work. In connection with her friend, Virginia Page, she has high hopes for using music to lift the lives of the inner city populace.

By the way, Philip, Rachel Winslow is an exceptionally beautiful woman. Rumor has it that she expects to be married this spring to Miss Page's brother. This young man was raised by those whom dear old Dr. Symmons used to call the idle rich. Maxfield has told me that the young man spent his days as an unproductive member of the country club set. But, the exciting news is that he was converted in a "down and outer's" mission meeting where his wife-to-be took an active part in the service. Just another example of the powerful acts of God that are at work in Raymond.

These are only a few illustrations of results in individual lives that are in obedience to the pledge. I meant to have spoken of President Marsh of Lincoln College. He is a graduate of my alma mater, and I knew him slightly when I was in my senior year. He has taken an active part in the recent city election and referendum campaign. His influence in the upcoming city election was large. He impressed me, as did all the other disciples in this movement, as having fought through some hard questions. All of them have taken up some real burdens that have caused and still do cause that suffering of which Henry Maxwell speaks. This is a suffering that does not eliminate, but actually intensifies, a positive and practical joy.

CHAPTER 20

I hope you are not becoming weary with this letter. I am unable to avoid the feeling of fascination which my entire stay here has encouraged. I want to tell you something of the meeting at Raymond's First Church today.

As I said, I heard Maxwell preach. At his earnest request, I had preached for him the Sunday before, and this was the first time I had heard him since the Association meeting four years ago. His sermon this morning was different from his earlier sermons. It was as if it had been preached by someone living on another planet. I was profoundly touched. I believe I actually shed tears once. Others in the congregation seemed to be affected in the same way. His text was: "What is that to you? Follow Me." It was a most unusual and impressive appeal to the Christians of Raymond to obey Jesus' teachings and follow in His steps regardless of what others might do. I cannot give you even the plan of the sermon. It would take too long. At the close of the service, there was the usual meeting that has become a regular feature of the First Church disciples. Into this meeting come all those who have made the pledge to do as Jesus would do, and the time is spent in mutual fellowship, confession, and questions as to what Jesus would do in special cases, and prayer that the one great guide of every disciple's conduct would be the Holy Spirit.

Maxwell asked me to come into this meeting. Nothing in all my ministry life, Philip, has so moved me. I have never felt the Spirit's presence so powerfully. It was a meeting of testimonies and of the most loving fellowship. I was irresistibly driven back to the first years of Christianity. There was something about all this that was apostolic in its simplicity and imitation of Christ.

I asked questions. One that seemed to arouse more interest than any other was in regard to the extent of the Christian disciple's sacrifice of personal property. Maxwell tells me that so far no one has interpreted the Spirit of Jesus in such a way as to abandon his earthly possessions, give away his wealth, or in any literal way imitate the Christians of the order, for example, of St. Francis of Assisi. It was the unanimous consent, however, that if any disciple should feel that Jesus in his own particular case would do that, there could be only one answer to the question. Maxwell admitted that he was still to a certain degree uncertain as to Jesus' probable action when it came to the details of each household, the possession of wealth, and the encouragement of certain luxuries. It is, however, very evident that many of these disciples have repeatedly carried their obedience to Jesus to the extreme limit, regardless of financial loss. There is no lack of courage or consistency at this point.

It is also true that some of the businessmen and women who took the pledge have lost great sums of money in this imitation of Jesus, and many have, like Alexander Powers, lost valuable positions owing to the impossibility of doing what they had been accustomed to doing and at the same time, what they felt Jesus would do in the same situation. Yet, many who have suffered in this way have been helped financially by those who still have means. In this regard, I think it is true that these disciples have all things in common. Certainly I can say that I have never seen such scenes in my church or in any other. I never dreamed that such Christian fellowship could exist in this age. I almost did not believe the witness of my own senses. I still ask myself if this is the close of the nineteenth century in America.

But now, dear friend, I come to the real cause of this letter, the real heart of the whole question that the First Church of Raymond has forced upon me. Before the meeting closed today, steps were taken to secure the cooperation of all other Christian disciples in this country. *He said as much to me one day when we were discussing the effect of this movement upon the Church in general.*

He said, "Suppose that the Church membership in general in this country made this pledge and lived up to it! What a revolution it would cause in Christendom! But why not? Is it any more than the disciple ought to do? Has he followed Jesus, unless he is willing to do this? Is the test of discipleship any less today than it was in Jesus' time?"

I do not know all that preceded or followed this thinking, but the idea crystallized today in a plan to secure the fellowship of all the Christians in America. The churches, through their pastors, will be asked to form disciple gatherings like the one in the First Church. Volunteers will be called for among the great body of church members in the United States, who will promise to do as Jesus would do. Maxwell spoke particularly of the result of such general action on the alcohol and tobacco question. He is terribly serious about this. He told me that there was no question in his mind that these unsavory opportunists would be beaten in Raymond at the election now near at hand. If so, they could go on with courage to do the redemptive work begun by the evangelist and now taken up by the disciples in his own church. If the alcohol and tobacco lobbies triumph again, there will be a terrible and, he thinks, unnecessary waste of Christian service. But, however we differ on that point, he has convinced his church that the time has come for fellowship with other Christians. Surely, if the First Church could work such changes in society and its surroundings, the Church in general by combining with such a fellowship, not of creed but of conduct, ought to stir the entire nation to a higher life and a new conception of Christian discipleship.

This is a grand idea, Philip, but right here is where I find myself hesitating. I do not deny that the Christian disciple ought to follow Christ's steps as closely as these here in Raymond have tried to do. But I cannot avoid asking what the result would be if I ask my church in Chicago to do it. I am writing this after feeling the solemn, profound touch of the Spirit's presence, and I confess to you, old friend, that I cannot call up in my church a dozen prominent business professionals whom I honestly believe would try this experiment at the risk of all they hold dear.

Can you do any better in your church? What are we to say? That the churches would not respond to the call: "Come and suffer?" Is our standard of Christian discipleship a wrong one? Or are we possibly deceiving ourselves, and would we be agreeably disappointed if we once asked our people to take such a pledge faithfully? The actual results of the pledge as obeyed here in Raymond are enough to make any pastor wonder, and at the same time, long that they might occur in his own congregation. Certainly I have never seen a church so totally blessed by the Spirit as this one. But—am I myself ready to take this pledge? I ask the question honestly, and I dread to face an honest answer. I know well enough that I should have to change a great deal in my life if I were to undertake to follow His steps so closely.

I have called myself a Christian for many years. For the past ten years, I have enjoyed a life that has included comparatively little suffering of any kind. I am, quite honestly, living at a long distance from city problems and the life of the impoverished, the downtrodden, and the abandoned. What would obedience to this pledge demand of me? I hesitate to answer. My church is wealthy, full of well-to-do, satisfied people. The standard of their discipleship is, quite frankly, not of a nature to respond to the call of suffering or personal loss. I say: "I am aware." I may be mistaken. I may have erred in not stirring their deeper commitment.

Philip, my friend, I have expressed my deepest thoughts to you. Shall I go back to my people next Sunday and stand up before them in my large city church and say: "Let us follow Jesus closer; let us walk in His steps where it will cost us something more than it is costing us now. Let us pledge not to do anything without first asking: 'What would Jesus do?'" If I should go before them with that message, it would be a strange and startling one to them. But why? Are we not ready to follow Him all the way? What is it to be a follower of Jesus? What does it mean to imitate Him? What does it mean to walk in His steps?

The Reverend Calvin Bruce, doctor of Divinity of the Nazareth Avenue Church, Chicago, let his pen fall on the table. He had come to the parting of the ways, and his question, he felt sure, was the question of many a man in the ministry and in the church. He went to his window and opened it. He was oppressed with the weight of his convictions and he felt almost suffocated with the air in the room. He wanted to see the stars and feel the fresh air of the outside world.

The night was very still. The clock in the First Church was just striking midnight. As it finished, a clear, strong voice down in the direction of the

Rectangle district came floating up to him as if born on radiant pinions.

It was a voice of one of Gray's old converts, a night watchman, who sometimes comforted his lonesome hours by a verse or two from some familiar hymn:

> *Must Jesus bear the cross alone*
> *And all the world go free?*
> *No, there's a cross for everyone,*
> *And there's a cross for me.*

The Reverend Calvin Bruce turned away from the window and, after a little hesitation, knelt. "What would Jesus do?" That was the burden of his prayer. Never had he yielded himself so completely to the Spirit's searching. He stayed on his knees a long time, and then climbed into bed. His sleep was troubled and he was awakened many times. He rose before it was clear dawn, and threw open his window again. As the light in the east grew stronger he repeated to himself: "What would Jesus do? Shall I follow in His steps?"

The sun rose and flooded the city with its power. When shall the dawn of a new discipleship bring the conquering triumph of a closer walk with Jesus? When shall Christendom follow more closely the path he made?

It is the way the Master trod;
Shall not the servant tread it still?

With this question throbbing through his whole being, the Reverend Calvin Bruce, doctor of Divinity, went back to Chicago, and the great crisis in his Christian life in the ministry suddenly came upon him.

CHAPTER 21

Teacher, I will follow you wherever you go.
Matthew 8:19

The Sunday afternoon orchestral matinee at Chicago's famed concert hall, *The Auditorium,* had just ended and the exiting crowd was dashing to taxis and parking garages. An attendant helped patrons into each car as it rolled to a stop at the curb and then plunged into the river of vehicles that surged under the elevated tracks, and finally up Michigan Avenue.

"Taxi!" shouted *The Auditorium* attendant. "Taxi! 624!" he repeated motioning the driver into position at the curb. Standing beside the attendant were two young women. One of the women climbed into the taxi, and the attendant continued to hold the door for the other, who stood hesitating on the curb.

"Come on, Felicia! What are you waiting for! I'm freezing!" urged the older woman.

The woman still on the curb reached into her beaded purse and took out a bill, which she handed to a ragged boy, shivering on the sidewalk next to her. He took the money with a look of astonishment, and a "Thanks, lady!" and quickly disappeared into the waiting crowd. The young woman stepped into the taxi, the attendant secured the door, and a few moments later, the driver was headed toward one of the palatial homes along the shore of Lake Michigan.

"You are always doing something strange like that, Felicia," said the first woman.

"Am I? What have I done now, Rose?" asked the other, looking up suddenly and turning her head toward her sister.

"Oh, giving money to that boy! He looked as if he needed a good hot bath and a meal more than your handout. I'm surprised you didn't invite him to come home with us. It wouldn't have surprised me a bit if you had. You're always doing such bizarre things."

"What would have been so wrong about taking in a boy like that and giving him a hot meal?" Felicia asked softly.

"I suppose 'strange' was the wrong word," replied Rose indifferently. "Let me put it to you as Madam Blanc would, 'Such things are simply not done, my dear Felicia!'" The older sister turned and looked out the window. "Oh, dear! I'm exhausted."

She yawned, and Felicia silently watched the scenery pass by.

"That concert was downright boring," Rose exclaimed, "and that Chinese—or whatever he was—violinist was the worst. I don't see how you could sit there looking as if you were enjoying yourself."

"I liked the music," answered Felicia quietly.

"You like anything. I've never known a person with so little critical taste."

Felicia felt her cheeks flush with annoyance, but she refused to respond. Rose yawned again, and then took out her compact and touched up her makeup.

"Do you want to know something?" she stated abruptly. "I'm sick of just about everything. I hope the play will be exciting tonight. Who's it by? Frank Lloyd Wright?"

"I believe you mean Andrew Lloyd Webber," corrected Felicia.

"Yes, Webber! He wrote 'Les Miserables.'"

"So what are we going to see?"

"I think 'The Shadows of London' at the Blackstone. It was a Broadway and London hit forever. You know we have a box with the Delanos tonight."

Felicia turned her face toward her sister. Her expressive brown eyes narrowed for a second.

"Rose, tonight we'll get sentimental over some touching music and a heart-tugging script, and yet we never weep over the real tragedies of life. What is 'Les Miserables' or 'Shadows of London' compared to the misery on State Street or almost anyplace in the Loop? Why can't we feel some passion for life as it really is?"

"Because real people can be so disagreeable and it's too much of a bother, I suppose," replied Rose carelessly. "Felicia, you're trying to change the world. What's the use? It's not our fault that some people are asked to live in poverty and misery. It has always been that way and it will always be that way. Let's just be thankful for what we have."

"Suppose Jesus had followed that principle," replied Felicia, with unusual persistence. "Do you remember Dr. Bruce's sermon a few Sundays ago—something about Christ becoming poor for our sakes."

"Of course, I remember," said Rose with annoyance. "But didn't Dr. Bruce go on to say that there's nothing wrong with having money as long as you are kind and try to help the less fortunate when you can?"

"Rose, that is exactly. . . ."

"And I'm sure Dr. Bruce is feeling no pain himself," interrupted Rose. "I'd be surprised if he gives up any of his goodies because some people don't have enough. What good would it do if he did?"

"What good would it do? I'll tell you. . . ."

Rose cut her off again, "Believe me, Felicia, there will always be rich folks and poor folks in this world. You can't change that. You know, ever since Rachel wrote and told you about all that strange business going on in Raymond, you have been on some kind of mission. People can't live on that emotional level all the time. Rachel will give it up soon enough if she's smart."

"I wish Rachel would come to Chicago," Felicia whispered thoughtfully. "I'd love to talk to her about what's going on in Raymond."

"It's a pity she won't let them book her at *The Auditorium.* Someone told me she received an offer. I'm going to write and ask her to come. I'm just dying to hear what all the fuss is about."

Felicia looked out of the window and said nothing. The taxi rolled on past two blocks of magnificent private residences and turned into one of the wide driveways and through a security gate.

Pulling up to the front, the driver jumped out and opened the back door for the sisters, who hurried up the steps and into the elegant stone house.

The owner of the house, Mr. Charles R. Sterling, sat before his fireplace reading. He had made his fortune in oil speculation and was said to be worth something over $50 million. Sterling's wife and Constance Winslow, Rachel's mother, were sisters. Mrs. Sterling had been an invalid for several years. The two girls, Rose and Felicia, were the Sterling's only children. Rose was twenty-one years old, pretty and vivacious. She had been well educated in the best schools, and yet she often seemed indifferent to life and her father was already saying about her, "She's a hard person to please."

Felicia was nineteen, with a dark, sophisticated beauty, quite the opposite of her cousin, Rachel. What Rose lacked in warmth and generosity, Felicia decidedly made up for. The younger sister was just now awakening to Christian concerns, which was a puzzlement to her father, and a source of irritation to her mother.

The sisters entered the library and greeted their father by perching on the arms of his chair and giving him a peck on the cheek. "There's a letter for you, Felicia," Mr. Sterling, teased. "It's up there on the mantel."

Felicia jumped up and snatched the letter from above the fireplace. "It's from Rachel," she announced tearing it open.

"Well, what's the latest news from Raymond?" asked Sterling, looking at his youngest with his customary half-shut eyes, an expression that always made Felicia feel as if he were studying her.

"Rachel says Dr. Bruce has been staying in Raymond for two Sundays and seems quite interested in Reverend Maxwell and his group of First Church disciples."

"What does Rachel say about herself?" asked Rose, who was stretched out on the sofa almost buried under a half dozen hand-stitched sofa pillows.

"She's still singing down in the Rectangle district. The evangelistic meetings are over now, but she still performs Gospel concerts in the storefront chapel. I hope her friend Virginia finishes the new building before that old chapel falls down around their ears."

"What a waste—performing in that old place— as if those people could appreciate her talent anyway," Rose interjected. "I must write her and find out when she can come to Chicago for a visit."

Mr. Sterling returned to his book, and Rose continued.

"I don't get it. Rachel could set Chicago on its ear with her voice. She already has an invitation to perform at *The Auditorium*. But no—there she is throwing her talent away on people who don't even know what they're hearing."

"Rachel won't come here unless she can sing and keep the pledge she made at the same time," responded Felicia, after a pause.

"What pledge?" Mr. Sterling asked, then quickly added, "Oh, yes, I know: that thing they did at First Church. Alexander Powers used to be a friend of mine. I've heard that pledge was the reason he resigned his management position at Raymond Steel and handed over damaging evidence to the Interstate Commerce Commission. There's been a lot of crazy stuff going on in Raymond this past year. I wonder what Dr. Bruce thinks of it all. I really should have a talk with him about it."

"He's back home now—I heard he's preaching tomorrow," said Felicia. "Perhaps he'll tell us something about it."

There was silence for a minute. Then Felicia asked abruptly, "What if he should propose a pledge like that at our church?"

"Who? What are you talking about?" asked her father a little sharply.

"Dr. Bruce—I said, what if he proposes a pledge like that at our church? What if Dr. Bruce were to ask all of us to take a pledge saying we would not to do a single thing without first asking, 'What would Jesus do?'"

"There's very little danger of that," said Rose, rising suddenly from the couch.

"It's very impractical," said Mr. Sterling shortly.

"I understand from Rachel's letter that the Raymond church is going to make an attempt to extend the idea of the discipleship pledge to other churches," Felicia added. And then she said to herself. *It isn't very likely, but it sure would shake up a lot of churches and the people in them.*

"Oh, well, let's have something to eat first!" announced Rose, walking into the dining room. Her father and Felicia followed, and the meal proceeded in silence. Mrs. Sterling had her meals served in her room. Mr. Sterling, who seemed particularly preoccupied ate very little and excused himself early. Although it was Saturday night, he remarked that he would have to make a late trip downtown on some special business.

"Don't you think Dad has been looking pretty upset lately?" asked Felicia once he was gone.

"Oh, I don't know! I haven't noticed anything unusual," replied Rose. After some silence she asked, "Are you going to the theater with me tonight, Felicia? Mrs. Delano will be here at seven thirty, and she will be hurt if you don't go."

"I'll go, but I don't care much about seeing the show. I can see enough misery and un-happiness without going to the theater."

"That's a pretty bitter remark for a nineteen-year-old woman to make," observed Rose. "But then you're a rather unusual person all the way around, Felicia. If you're going up to see Mother, tell her I'll come when we get back from the theater, if she's still awake."

Felicia stayed with her mother until the driver arrived to take them to the theater. Mrs. Sterling was worried about her husband, and she talked incessantly, finding fault with every remark Felicia made. She would not listen to Felicia's attempts to read even a part of Rachel's letter, and when Felicia offered to stay with her for the evening, she flatly refused the offer.

CHAPTER 22

Felicia joined her sister but said little during their ride to the Blackstone. Arriving at the theater, they were met by Mrs. Delano and were ushered to their host's reserved seating. At intermission when Felicia declined to join the others, Mrs. Delano stayed back and tried to draw her out, but sensing resistance backed away. As something of a modern-day "chaperone" for half a dozen wealthy young women, she knew Felicia well enough to understand that she was a unique young person with a lot on her mind.

Though surrounded by a sea of bodies, Felicia was alone with her thoughts and emotions. She was struggling to shake off the feeling that she was on the verge of great crisis.

The musical was one of the most popular in the country. Besides the London and New York productions, touring companies criss-crossed North America taking the show to the general audience everywhere. There was one scene in the third act that impressed even Rose Sterling.

The first scene opened, it was midnight on Blackfriars Bridge. The Thames flowed dark and forbidding below. St. Paul's rose through the dim imposing light, its dome seeming to float above the buildings surrounding it. The figure of a child came upon the bridge and stood there for a moment looking around as if trying to find someone. Along the railing, about halfway across, a woman stood, leaning out over the edge. The audience immediately sensed the drama of the moment. The woman was about to jump. Just as she was stepping up to the parapet to throw herself into the river, the child caught sight of her, ran forward, and seized her dress, pulling her back from the edge. The woman was costumed in hideous rags and poverty.

The next scene was the interior of a slum tenement in the east side of London, a location well-known to London's homeless and outcast population. The rags, the overcrowding, the vileness, the horrible animal existence forced upon creatures made in God's image were so skillfully shown in this scene that many of the people in the theater caught themselves shrinking back a little as if contamination were possible from the nearness of it all. It was almost too realistic, and yet it had a horrible fascination for Felicia sitting there, buried deep in a cushioned seat and absorbed in thoughts that extended far beyond the dialogue on the stage.

From the tenement scene, the play shifted to the interior of a manor house, and an almost audible sigh of relief went up all over the auditorium. The contrast was startling. While the play continued, Felicia forgot plotting and clever lines. Instead she wrestled with the play's contrasts—rich and poor. The young woman found herself reliving over and over again, the scenes on the bridge and in the slums. She had never philosophized much about the cause of human misery: she was probably too young. But of late she had been intensely moved by the plight of the poor. This play only intensified her concern. It was this growing concern that made Rose call her "strange," and other people in her circle of friends call her "most unusual."

Felicia was struggling with the ageless human dilemma of reconciling extreme wealth and extreme poverty. How she would settle the matter in her own mind would ultimately transform her into a woman of rare love and self-sacrifice or a miserable puzzle to herself and all who knew her.

"Come on, Felicia, the play's over. Are you planning to go home or sit here all night?" asked Rose. Sure enough, the curtain was down and people were exiting the theater. They laughed and gossiped as if the emotional content of *The*

Shadows of London was simply clever diversion, with no relevance to anyone present.

Felicia rose and quietly went out into the hall behind the boxes. She was still so absorbed that she could not remember how the play production ended. In truth, it wasn't uncommon for Felicia to think herself into a fog that made her oblivious to anything going on around her—even in the midst of a crowd.

"Well, what did you think of it?" Rose asked when the sisters were walking up the steps to the front door. Though she seldom expressed it, she did appreciate her sister's observations concerning things.

"I thought it was a pretty fair picture of real life."

"I mean the acting," said Rose, annoyed.

"The bridge scene was well acted, especially the woman's part. I thought the man overdid the sentiment a little."

"Did you? I enjoyed that. And wasn't the scene between the two cousins funny when they first learned they were related. But the slum scene was horrible. I don't think they ought to show such things in a play. They're too painful."

"They must be painful in real life, too," replied Felicia.

"Yes, but we don't have to look at the real thing. That's why we see it at the theater, silly."

Rose went into the kitchen and fixed them a snack from a plate of fruit in the refrigerator.

"Are you going up to see Mother?" asked Felicia after a while.

"No," replied Rose, "if you go up, tell her I'm too tired to be pleasant."

So Felicia climbed the staircase and walked slowly down the upper hall to the door of her mother's bedroom. She gently knocked, and was quietly invited in by Mrs. Sterling's nurse. A shaded night-light was burning next to the bed.

"Clara, could you leave us alone for a few minutes," Mrs. Sterling asked as Felicia walked to the bed.

Felicia was surprised, but did not object. Instead, she leaned down and kissed her mother's forehead and asked how she was feeling.

"Felicia," said her mother, "would you pray for me?"

The question surprised her; it was so unlike any her mother had ever asked before, but she answered:

"Of course, mother, but what's wrong?"

"Felicia, I'm frightened. Your father—I have had such strange fears about him all day. Something is wrong, I just know it. I want you to pray." Mrs. Sterling's eyes were pained and pleading.

"Do you mean right now, Mother?"

"Yes, sweetheart. Pray."

Felicia reached out and took her mother's hand. It was trembling. Mrs. Sterling had never shown such tenderness for her younger daughter, and her strange demand now was the first real sign of any confidence in Felicia's character.

The young woman knelt beside the bed still holding her mother's fragile hand, and prayed. It is doubtful if she had ever prayed aloud before, but she must have said the right words because when she finished, her mother was weeping softly and her nervousness had passed.

Felicia sat on the edge of the bed for some time. When she was certain that her mother no longer needed her, she stood to go.

"Good night, Mother. You must let Clara call me if you feel upset during the night."

"I feel better now." Then as Felicia was moving away, Mrs. Sterling said: "Won't you kiss me goodnight, Felicia?"

Felicia went back and bent over her mother. As she left the room, her cheeks were wet with tears. She had seldom cried since she was a little child.

Sunday morning at the Sterling home was generally quiet. The girls usually attended Nazarene Avenue's eleven o'clock service. Mr. Sterling was not a member but a heavy contributor, and he usually attended the morning service as well. This time he did not come down to breakfast, and finally sent word by a servant that he did not feel well enough to go out. So Rose and Felicia drove to church alone.

When Dr. Bruce entered the pulpit to read the call to worship, those who knew him well did not detect anything unusual in his manner. He proceeded with the service as he always did. He was calm and his voice was steady and firm. His prayer was the first inkling the people had of anything new or strange. It is safe to say that the Nazareth Avenue Church had never before heard Dr. Bruce offer such a prayer anytime during his twelve years in the pulpit. They wondered what exactly had happened during his visit to Raymond. But, they could not have guessed that their minister had witnessed a revolution in the lives of a group of Christian disciples that had completely and permanently altered his definition of what it meant to follow Christ.

No one in Nazareth Avenue Church had any idea that the Reverend Calvin Bruce, D.D. —the dignified, cultured, refined doctor of Divinity, had just a few days earlier been on his knees crying like a little child; asking for strength and courage and a Christlikeness that would be evident in his Sunday message. That morning prayer was an involuntary disclosure of what his soul had so recently experienced.

In the hush that followed the prayer, a distinct wave of spiritual power moved over the congregation. Even the most insensitive persons in the church sensed it. Felicia's sensitivity to spiritual things caused her to respond swiftly with an eager anticipation of what was to follow. She was not alone in that regard. There was something in Dr. Bruce's prayer that stirred many disciples in that church. All over the sanctuary men and women leaned forward with interest as their minister began to give an account of his visit to Raymond. Dr. Bruce sensed that his people were responding to the same spirit he had felt in Raymond, and it filled him with hope that a spiritual baptism such as he had never experienced in all his ministry would be poured out in that place.

CHAPTER 23

"I have just returned from a visit to Raymond," Dr. Bruce began, "and I want to tell you something of my impressions of what's happening there."

The minister paused and looked with deep yearning at his people. At the same time, he experienced a great uncertainty of heart. How many of his wealthy and comfort-loving members could truly appreciate what he would be attempting to describe to them in his morning message? He had no idea how they would respond to his words. Nevertheless, he had been through his personal desert, and had come out of it ready to put his hand to the task.

After a brief pause, Pastor Bruce began to relate the story of the Raymond First Church experiment. The people already knew something of what was going on. The whole country had watched the progress of the disciples' pledges from television reports and even news magazines. When Reverend Maxwell decided that the time had come to invite the fellowship of other churches throughout the country, the national press and Edward Norman's television stations carried the stories. The new discipleship emphasis in Raymond had proven to be so effective that he wanted other churches to share in the blessings. A volunteer movement had already begun in a number of urban churches across the U.S. and Canada. These sprung up simply as a result of the earnest desire of certain individuals to walk closer in the steps of Jesus. Youth groups of every description had enthusiastically taken the discipleship pledge. Reports of miraculous change and empowerment began to pour into Raymond. This was a major boost for First Church disciples and seemed like a new birth for church members everywhere.

Dr. Bruce related the First Church story in all its simplicity and with an unusual personal interest that paved the way for the announcement that followed. Felicia listened to every word with trained attention. She sat mesmerized beside Rose. The moving testimony of God's grace thrilled her to tears. In contrast, Rose listened as if she were hearing an interesting story rather than the miracle of God at work.

"Dear friends," the minister said with emotion, "I am going to ask Nazareth Avenue Church to prayerfully consider taking the same pledge that the First Church of Raymond has taken. I know what this step can mean to you and me. It will necessitate a complete change of many of our habits. It will mean, possibly, being looked down upon by our sophisticated friends. I'm sure for some of us, it will mean financial loss. It can certainly mean that almost all of you will suffer some sort of hardship. I can guarantee that following Jesus in this way will provide all of us with a first century Christian experience. That means suffering, loss, hardship, and separation from everything un-Christlike. The test of discipleship is the same now as then. Those of us who pledge to do as Jesus would do, are simply promising to walk in His steps as He commands."

Again the minister paused, and surveyed his people. The result of his announcement was plainly visible in the stir that went across the congregation. He added in a quiet voice that all those who wished to make the pledge should remain after the morning service.

Without further announcements, Dr. Bruce launched into his sermon. His text was, "Teacher, I will follow You wherever You go." It was a sermon that touched the will, which, he noted, in turn should affect decisions of conduct. To hear what their minister had experienced was a revelation to the membership. It made them think of first century Christianity. Above all, it stirred them to consider the true meaning and purpose of church membership. This was the kind of sermon a man might preach once in a lifetime, and it contained enough truth to last for a long time to come.

The service closed in a hush that hovered over the congregation. Gradually people began to stand a few at a time. Some out of a sense of reverence seemed reluctant to move. Rose, however, walked straight out of the pew, and as she reached the aisle, turned her head and beckoned to Felicia who was still seated. By that time, the congregation was rising all over the church.

"I am going to stay," Felicia said. Rose recognized that tone of voice, and knew that it was fruitless to try and change her mind. Nevertheless she went back into the pew and faced her.

"Felicia," she whispered, and there was a flush of anger on her cheeks, "this isn't for us. You could embarrass our family. Besides, what will father say? Come on. Let's go home!"

Felicia looked at her but did not answer immediately. She shook her head.

"No, I'm going to stay. I want to take the discipleship pledge. I'm ready to obey it. Rose, you really have no idea why I am doing this, do you?" she remarked quietly.

Rose gave her sister a final look and then turned and walked back to the aisle. She didn't even stop to talk to her friends—no one except for Mrs. Delano, who was standing outside on the steps.

"So you are not going to volunteer to become one of Dr. Bruce's disciples?" Mrs. Delano asked, in a strange tone that embarrassed Rose.

"No, are you? I think it's absolutely absurd. I think those people in Raymond are fanatics. You know my cousin Rachel keeps us posted on what's happening."

"Yes, I understand that in many cases, it's resulting in serious hardship. From my point of view, I believe Dr. Bruce has simply gotten excited about a proposition that will split our church. You'll see that I'm right about this matter. There are scores of people in the church whose circumstances won't allow them to take such a pledge and keep it. I'm one of them," added Mrs. Delano as she stepped onto the sidewalk and was caught up in the crowd moving to the parking area.

When Rose reached home, her father was sitting in front of the fireplace reading.

"Where is Felicia?" he asked as Rose came in.

"She stayed for a meeting after the service," she replied curtly. Throwing off her coat she started upstairs, but Mr. Sterling called up to her.

"A meeting after the service? What do you mean?"

"Dr. Bruce asked the church to take the Raymond discipleship pledge."

Mr. Sterling looked up and closed his book.

"I didn't expect that of Dr. Bruce. Did many of the members stay?"

"I don't know. I didn't," replied Rose, and she went on upstairs leaving her father alone to interpret her news.

After throwing another log on the fire, he went to the window and watched as a jogger and a few cars passed on the street. A few minutes later, Mr. Sterling went into the dining room for Sunday dinner. Rose also came downstairs in time to hear her father instruct the cook not to serve dinner until Felicia returned from church.

Rose and her father returned to the study, where Mr. Sterling continued to pace nervously, and finally threw himself into a leather chair to brood. Rose, hearing her sister come in at last, met her in the hallway.

"How many stayed to take the pledge?" Rose asked curiously.

"About a hundred," replied Felicia heading toward the stairs. Mr. Sterling, standing in the door of his office, looked surprised. Felicia had been deeply affected by the meeting from which she had just come. However, it had been such an emotional and personal experience that she was not yet ready to discuss it with anyone. She was on the second step when her father called after her.

"Do you really mean to keep the pledge?" he asked.

Felicia looked troubled. "You wouldn't ask that question, Father, if you'd been at the meeting."

"We've been waiting dinner," he responded. Felicia slipped into the hall restroom to wash her hands, and then, joined her father and sister as they were served their meal. No one spoke. When she finished, Felicia excused herself and went up to see her mother.

No one but the two women knew what the conversation between Felicia and her mother was about. It is certain that Felicia told her mother about the great surge of spiritual power that had awed every person in the meeting after the service. It is also certain that Felicia had never before in her life experienced such a manifestation of God's love and power. Encouraged by the prayer she and her mother had shared the night before, Felicia opened her heart and told her mother everything.

Despite their prodding, Felicia was more reluctant to describe her experience to her father and sister. It was the same reluctance one might feel to describe a wonderful sunset to a person who never talked about anything but the most trivial matters.

When that Sunday in the Sterling household was drawing to a close and there was a soft glow of warm lights, Felicia returned to her room and knelt at a chair praying. When she said, "Amen," and raised her face toward the light, it was the face of a woman who had already defined for herself the issues of life with which she would have to deal.

That same evening in the Nazareth Avenue Church parsonage, Dr. Bruce discussed the events of the day with his wife. They were of one heart and mind in the matter and faced their new future with all the faith and courage of new disciples. Neither was deceived as to the probable consequences of the pledge to themselves or to the church.

They had been talking just a little while when the front doorbell rang.

"Well, Edward Lawlor! Come in," he said to the caller as he opened the door.

A commanding figure in a black suit stepped into the hall. Bishop Lawlor was extraordinarily tall and possessed broad shoulders. The impression he made on strangers was, first, that of great energy, and then of great affection for others.

Coming into the living room Lawlor greeted Mrs. Bruce, who after a few moments stepped out of the room, leaving the two men to speak privately. The Bishop sat in a comfortable easy chair before the open fire. There was just enough dampness in the early spring of the year to make the fire pleasant.

"Calvin, you have taken a very serious step today," he finally said, lifting his large dark eyes to his old college classmate's face. "I heard about your service this afternoon. I couldn't resist coming by to ask you about it tonight."

"I'm glad you came, Edward." Dr. Bruce laid a hand on the Bishop's shoulder. "You understand what all of this means?"

"I think I do. Yes, I am sure I do." The Bishop spoke thoughtfully. He sat with his hands clasped together. It seemed a shadow crept over his face, which was marked with the lines of consecrated service and love for humanity. Again he lifted his eyes toward his old friend.

"Calvin, we have always understood each other. Even though our paths led us to different church traditions, we have walked together in Christian fellowship."

"That's true, Edward," replied Dr. Bruce with an emotion he made no attempt to conceal or subdue. "Thank God for it. I treasure your friendship and guidance more than any other man's, though it has always been more than I deserve."

The Bishop looked affectionately at his friend. But the shadow still rested on his face. After a pause he spoke again:

"The new discipleship will mean a crisis for you in your work. If you keep this pledge to do all things as Jesus would do—as I know you will—it doesn't take a prophet to predict some remarkable changes in your church." The Bishop looked wistfully at his friend and then continued. "In fact, I do not see how any church can remain status quo after taking the Raymond pledge and living it out." He paused as if he were waiting for his friend to say something, to ask some question. But Bruce was not aware of the fire that burned in the Bishop's heart over the very question that he and Henry Maxwell had decided to pursue.

"Now, in my denomination for instance," continued the Bishop, "it would be rather a difficult matter, I fear, to find very many people who would take a discipleship pledge like that and live up to it. Martyrdom is a lost art with us. Our brand of Christianity loves its ease and comfort too well to take up anything so rough and heavy as a cross. And yet what does following Jesus mean? What is it to walk in His steps?"

The Bishop was talking to himself now, and for a moment, he even seemed to forget his friend's presence. For the first time there flashed into Dr. Bruce's mind a suspicion of the truth. *What if the Bishop would throw the weight of his great influence on the side of the Raymond movement? He had the following of the most aristocratic, wealthy people, not only in Chicago, but in several other large cities in the state. What if the Bishop joined with them as they pursued this new form of discipleship!*

His thoughts were about to be transcribed into audible words. With the familiarity of lifelong friendship, Dr. Bruce had just placed his hand on the Bishop's shoulder and was about to ask a very important question, when the phone rang. Dr. Bruce moved to answer the phone in his office but stopped when he realized his wife had answered it in the hall. Before he could resume his thought, he heard her scream and call out his name. Dr. Bruce and the Bishop jumped to their feet and met Mrs. Bruce in the hallway. Her face was white and she was trembling.

"Oh, Calvin! Such terrible news! It's Mr. Sterling. . . . What a blow to those girls!"

"What is it?" Dr. Bruce said as she handed him the phone.

"Mr. Sterling shot himself a few minutes ago. He killed himself in his bedroom. Mrs. Sterling . . ."

"I will be right over," Dr. Bruce assured the caller.

"Would you go with me?" he asked the Bishop. "The Sterlings are old friends of yours, aren't they?"

The Bishop was very pale, but as always, quite calm. He looked his friend in the face, then answered.

"Yes, Calvin, of course. I will go with you as you undertake this crisis at the Sterling's, and I will also walk with you as you undertake your new venture."

And even in that moment of horror at the unexpected news, Dr. Bruce understood what the Bishop had promised to do.

CHAPTER 24

They follow the Lamb wherever he goes.
Revelation 14:4

When Dr. Bruce and the Bishop drove up to the Sterling home, they found everything in the usually well-appointed household in a state of great confusion. An ambulance and two police cars, with lights flashing, were parked in the drive. They hurried up the front steps and into the foyer to find that the downstairs rooms were virtually empty. All the activity seemed to be concentrated upstairs and they could hear frantic voices and strange noises coming from the second floor. One of the servants ran down the front staircase with a look of horror on her face just as the Bishop and Dr. Bruce were heading up.

"Felicia is upstairs with Mrs. Sterling," the servant whispered in answer to a question, and then burst into tears.

Felicia met the two men at the top of the stairs. She immediately turned to Dr. Bruce and put both her hands in his. The Bishop then laid his hand on her shoulder and the three stood there a moment in perfect silence. The Bishop had known Felicia since she was a child. He was the first to break the silence.

"The God of all mercy be with you, Felicia, in this dark hour. How is your mother—"

The Bishop hesitated. Out of the buried past, he suddenly remembered a tender romance in his early manhood. Not even Bruce knew about it. There had been a time when the Bishop thought he was in love with the beautiful Camilla Rolfe. But, she had given her heart to a young man named Sterling instead. The Bishop carried no bitterness with that memory, but he remembered.

In response to the Bishop's unfinished question, Felicia turned and went back to the door of her mother's room. She had not said a word yet, but both men were struck with her astonishing sense of peace. She beckoned for them to follow, and the two ministers entered the room with an unmistakable feeling that they were about to witness something very unusual.

Rose lay upon the bed with her arms outstretched. Clara, her longtime nurse, sat quietly sobbing. And Mrs. Sterling with luminous light radiating on her face, lay in bed so still that she seemed only to be asleep. Then, for the first time, the men comprehended the truth. The beautiful Mrs. Sterling lay dead in her bed, and her husband lay dead in the next room. The sight of Camilla Sterling somehow provided Bishop Lawlor a calmness and strength that the children of God are often able to possess in a time of crisis. And he used that calmness and strength well in the days that followed.

A few moments later, Dr. Bruce looked down from the upstairs window and noticed four or five reporters and a television news crew standing on the lawn. A police officer blocked their entry into the house. Stepping back into the hallway, Dr. Bruce and the Bishop were told the facts of the "Sterling tragedy," as it would later be called by the newscasters.

Mr. Sterling had gone up to his room about nine o'clock, and from all accounts that was the last time he was seen until the sound of a single gunshot brought the maid running into his bedroom. When she saw Mr. Sterling lying dead on the floor with his pistol still clutched in his hand, she walked purposefully to the bedside table, picked up the phone, and dialed 911. At the time of their father's suicide, Felicia was sitting next to her mother's bed, and Rose was reading in her room. Both heard the shot and ran to his bedroom only to be pushed back by the maid. Then, in a state of total terror, they returned to their mother's bedroom, where they flung themselves down at the foot of the bed. Mrs. Sterling at first could not comprehend what had happened. When she did come to her senses, she insisted that someone call Dr. Bruce immediately and ask him to come. She had then insisted on seeing her husband. In spite of Felicia's efforts, Mrs. Sterling, summoning all her strength and supported by Clara, walked down the hall and into the room where her husband lay. She looked at him with a tearless face, then returned to her own room and collapsed onto the bed. Just as Dr. Bruce and the Bishop entered the house, she died with a prayer of forgiveness for herself and for her husband on her lips, Felicia bending over her, and Rose still lying senseless at her feet.

Death had intruded swiftly and unashamedly into the Sterling's lavish lifestyle that Sunday night, but the full extent of the tragedy was not learned until the facts in regard to Mr. Sterling's business affairs were finally disclosed.

Then it was learned that Mr. Sterling was facing financial ruin due to a series of failed investments that had in a few short months swept away the bulk of his supposed fortune. Sterling was a cunning and desperate man who battled for his very life when he realized what was happening. But, on that fateful Sunday afternoon, he had received news that proved conclusively that he had lost his struggle. In fact, his fortune had been a reality only on paper and when real money, cold hard cash was required to support the failing enterprises, none could be produced.

Sterling's sense of well-being rested on a veneer of deceit and speculation that had no foundation in moral values. He knew that fact better than anyone else, but had hoped, with the hope such men always have, that the same methods that brought him the money would also prevent the loss. He had been deceived in this fantasy as many others have been. As soon as the truth that he was practically a beggar had dawned upon him, he felt there was but one way out—suicide. This ending was the natural result of the life that he had lived. He had made money his god. As soon as that god left his little world, there was nothing more to worship; and when a man's object of worship is gone, he has nothing to live for at all.

Mr. Sterling's sudden death and the manner in which he died were too great a shock for a person in Mrs. Sterling's condition to bear. Her husband had not taken her into his confidence for years, but she knew that the source of his wealth was shaky. Her life had been filled with worry for some time. Her family, the Rolfes, always gave the impression that they could endure more disaster than anyone else. Mrs. Sterling demonstrated the old family tradition when she walked into the room where her husband lay. But her feeble body could not stand the shock, and quickly rebelled, giving up after long years of suffering and disappointment.

This triple blow, the death of father and mother, and the loss of their wealth, had an unmistakable effect on the sisters. The horror of the events left Rose in shock for weeks. She lay on her bed silent and unmoved by the sympathy of anyone around her. She did not seem to realize yet that the money which had been so great a part of her very identity was gone. Even when she was told that she and Felicia must leave the house, she did not seem to understand what was meant.

Felicia, however, was fully aware of the implications. She knew just what had happened and why. She began discussing her future with her cousin Rachel just a few hours after the funerals. Mrs. Winslow and Rachel had come to Chicago as soon as the terrible news had reached them, and with other friends of the family, were helping to assess Rose and Felicia's options.

"Felicia, you and Rose must come back to Raymond with us," decided Rachel. "As far as we're concerned, it's settled. Mother and I will not take no for an answer." Rachel's love for her cousins was deepened by the knowledge that they both now had given themselves to the new discipleship of doing what Jesus would do.

"Unless I can find something to do here," answered Felicia.

"What could you do, dear?"

"Find a job I suppose. I haven't finished college, but I'm sure I can find something. I have learned to cook a little," Felicia added with a slight smile.

"Then you can cook for us. Mother is always having trouble in her kitchen," Rachel teased in an effort to break the tension. "You and Rose can both transfer to the University in Raymond and live with us."

"That may be our only realistic option," Felicia responded. "I'm willing to do anything necessary to finish my education, and I could also use a hand with Rose. She may never get over the shock of all this."

"We will arrange the details when we get to Raymond," Rachel said, smiling through her tears at Felicia's eager willingness to leave behind the only life she had ever known.

In a few weeks Rose and Felicia found themselves a part of the Winslow family in Raymond. It was a bitter experience for Rose, but there was nothing else for her to do. She accepted the inevitable, brooding over the great change in her life and adding to her sister's already heavy burden.

The good news was that Felicia at once found herself in an atmosphere of discipleship that was like heaven to her. It is true that Mrs. Winslow was not in sympathy with the course that Rachel was taking, but the remarkable events in Raymond since the discipleship pledge was taken were too impressive even for her to deny. With Rachel, Felicia found perfect fellowship. She almost immediately found a way she could help at the Rectangle Center. It had not taken long for Felicia to become aware of the demands of running a household and was eager to help with whatever needed to be done. In a short time, she demonstrated a real talent and enjoyment for the art of cooking. Virginia was so impressed that she asked her to supervise the kitchen at the Center.

Felicia entered upon this work with great pleasure. For the first time in her life, she had the delight of doing something of value for the happiness of others. Her resolve to do everything after asking, "What would Jesus do?" touched her to the very core. She began to develop and strengthen wonderfully. Even Mrs. Winslow was obliged to acknowledge the great beauty of Felicia's character. Her aunt looked with astonishment upon her niece, this city-bred girl, the daughter of a millionaire, now walking around in her kitchen, her arms covered with flour and occasionally a streak of it across her face. At first Felicia had a habit of rubbing her nose forgetfully when she was trying to remember some recipe, mixing various dishes with the greatest interest, washing up pans and kettles, and doing what she had once considered to be the ordinary work of a servant.

"Felicia, I cannot allow you to do all the cooking for us and the Rectangle Center. How do you find time for your studies?"

"What's wrong? Don't you like the muffins I made this morning?" Felicia would ask meekly, but with a hidden smile, knowing her aunt's weakness for her creations.

"They were wonderful, Felicia. But it doesn't seem right for you to be doing so much."

"Why not? I'm keeping up with my studies."

Her aunt looked at her thoughtfully, noting her sincerity.

"Felicia, have you considered what you would like to pursue once you graduate from the university?" her aunt asked.

"Since you asked," Felicia offered, "I do have a dream. One day, I would like to open a cooking shop in Chicago or some other large city. I would also like to volunteer to work with young mothers living in the poorer areas, teaching them about nutrition, what to buy with their food stamps, and how to properly prepare meals.

"I remember hearing Dr. Bruce say once that he believed one of the great miseries of poverty included poor food. He even went so far as to say that he thought some kinds of crime could be traced to poor nutrition. I've given this a lot of thought, and I believe I could make a good living through the shop and at the same time, help Rose and others."

Felicia pondered this dream until it became a reality. Meanwhile she grew in her devotion to the people of the Rectangle district, who affectionately called her the "angel cook." Underneath a beautiful character was growing, and she was always reminded of her promise made in Nazareth Avenue Church. "What would Jesus do?" She prayed and hoped and worked and ordered her life by the answer to that question. It inspired her life and her ambition.

CHAPTER 25

Almost a year had passed since the Sunday morning Dr. Bruce came into his pulpit with the message of this new form of discipleship—a year of great excitement in Nazareth Avenue Church. Never before had Reverend Calvin Bruce realized the depth of feeling he had for his members. He humbly confessed that the appeal had met with an unexpected response from men and women who, like Felicia, were hungry for something in their lives that conventional church fellowship had failed to give them.

However, Dr. Bruce was not yet satisfied with himself in this regard. He met with his friend, the Bishop, and the two sat in Dr. Bruce's study talking once again.

"You know what I have come for this evening?" the Bishop was saying after a lengthy discussion of results and consequences of the pledge taken by the Nazareth Avenue people.

Dr. Bruce looked over at the Bishop and shook his head.

"I have come to confess that I have not yet kept my promise to walk in His steps in the way that I believe I should if I am to satisfy my own commitment to walk in His steps."

Dr. Bruce had risen and was pacing back and forth across his study. The Bishop remained in the deep easy chair with his hands folded, but his eyes burned with the glow that was characteristic before he made some great decision.

"Edward," Dr. Bruce spoke abruptly, "I am not yet satisfied with myself either. But, I have at last decided on a specific plan to fulfill my pledge to follow in the steps of Jesus. My difficulty is that in order to initiate my plan, I must first resign from Nazareth Avenue Church."

"I knew you would," replied the Bishop quietly. "And I came in this evening to say that I shall be called to do the same thing with my ministry."

Dr. Bruce turned and walked up to his friend. They both had a repressed excitement.

"Is it necessary in your case?" asked Bruce.

"Yes. Let me state my reasons. Probably they are the same as yours. In fact, I am sure they are." The Bishop paused a moment, then went on with increasing emotion.

"Calvin, I do not mean to say that my life has been completely free from burdens or sorrow, but

312

I have certainly led what some would call a comfortable and even luxurious life. I live in a beautiful home, drive an expensive car, eat whatever I like, wear fine clothing, and travel whenever and wherever I please. I suppose I have been to Europe at least a dozen times. I have been privileged to enjoy the most beautiful art, literature, and music. In truth, I have no understanding of what it means to do without.

"Lately, I have been unable to silence the question, 'What have I suffered for the sake of Christ?' Paul was told what great things he must suffer for the sake of his Lord. Maxwell's position at Raymond is well taken when he insists that to walk in the steps of Christ means to suffer. When have I suffered or been called to sacrifice? The petty trials and annoyances of my pastoral life are not worth mentioning as sorrows or sufferings. Compared with Paul or any of the Christian martyrs or early disciples, I have lived a life so extravagant that it borders on sinfulness. Frankly, this is not my idea of walking in the steps of Jesus. In my present position, I see no opportunity to give more of my life to the actual physical and spiritual needs of the desperate people in the worst part of this city."

The Bishop had risen now and walked over to the window. The street in front of the house was as bright as day, and he looked out at cars passing on the street, then turned and made a passionate statement that showed how deep the volcanic fire in him burned:

"Calvin, this city is filled to overflowing with misery, sin, selfishness, and despair. It saddens my heart. And I have struggled for years with the sickening awareness that some day I would be asked to leave the comfort of my present surroundings and put my life on the line for the sake of others. With so much need before me, how can I continue to sit back and be little more than a contented freeloader? I have heard the words of Jesus many times lately, *Whatever you did not do for one of the least of these, you did not do for me* (Matthew 25:45). And I ask myself, when have I personally visited the prisoner or the desperate or the sinful in any way that has actually caused me suffering? Instead, I have followed the conventional soft habits of my social status and have lived in the company of my affluent and refined church members. What have I suffered for Jesus' sake? Do you know, Calvin," he turned abruptly toward his friend, "I have been tempted lately to lash myself with a scourge. If I had lived in Martin Luther's time, I should have bared my back to a self-inflicted torture."

The dramatic mental image of the Bishop's final comment brought a quick smile to Dr. Bruce's face, but only for a second. Never had he seen the Bishop or heard him speak as passionately. There was a sudden silence in the room. The Bishop sat down again and bowed his head.

Dr. Bruce spoke at last:

"Edward, you have expressed my feelings also. I have been in a similar position for years. My life has been one of comparative ease. I do not, of course, mean to say that I have not had trials and discouragements and burdens in my church ministry. But I cannot say that I have suffered any hardships for Jesus either. That verse in Peter constantly haunts me, *Christ suffered for you, leaving you an example, that you should follow in his steps* (1 Peter 2:21). I have lived in luxury. I do not know what it means to be in want. I also have had leisure for travel and pleasurable companionship. I have been surrounded by the soft, easy comforts of civilized society. The sin and misery of this great city have beaten like waves against the stone walls of my church and of this house in which I live, and I have hardly noticed them; the walls have been so thick. I have reached the point where I cannot endure any longer.

"I am not condemning our church because I love the people I serve. Nor am I forsaking the Church. I believe in its mission and have no desire to destroy it. Least of all do I desire to abandon my Christian fellowship. But I feel that I must resign my position as pastor of Nazareth Church in order to be satisfied that I am walking as I ought to walk in His steps. In this action, I judge no other minister and pass no criticism on others' discipleship. But I feel as you do. I must come personally into a close contact with the sin and shame and degradation of this great city. And I know that to do that I must sever my immediate connection with Nazareth Avenue Church. I do not see any other way."

Again a silence fell over the two men. It was no ordinary action they were embarking upon. They had both reached the same conclusion by the same reasoning and they were too knowledgeable to underestimate the seriousness of their position.

"What is your plan?" the Bishop asked at last, looking with the smile that always lit up his face.

"My plan," replied Dr. Bruce slowly, "is, in brief, to put myself into the center of the greatest human need I can find in this city. By that, I mean I am prepared to live there. My wife is fully in agreement. We have already decided to find a residence in that part of the city where we can make our personal lives count for the most."

"Let me suggest a place." The Bishop was on fire now. His fine face actually glowed with the enthusiasm of the movement in which he and his friend were now personally involved. He proceeded to unfold a plan of such far-reaching power and possibility that Dr. Bruce, capable and experienced as he was, was amazed at the vision of a greater soul.

They sat up late and appeared so excited that an observer might have thought they were planning a trip to explore some far-off land. The Bishop said many times afterward that the moment his decision was reached to live a life of personal sacrifice, he suddenly felt uplifted, as if a great burden had been taken from his shoulders. He was overjoyed. So was Dr. Bruce for the same reason.

Their plan as it finally grew into a workable strategy was in reality nothing more than the renting of a large building formerly used as a brewery warehouse. The building was to be reconfigured to provide for their housing in the very heart of the city where the bars ruled with strength, the tenements were their filthiest, and shame, and poverty were manifested in their most hideous forms. This was not a new idea. It was the teaching started by Jesus Christ when He left His Father's house and forsook the riches that were His in order to get nearer to humanity and, by becoming identified with its sin, helped to draw humanity away from its sin to new life. Their plan was as old as Bethlehem and Nazareth. And in this particular case, it was the best approach to satisfy the hunger these two men had to suffer for Christ.

They had a longing that had reached a passion, to get nearer to the great physical poverty and spiritual decay of the mighty city that throbbed around them. How could they do this without becoming a part of it as nearly as one person can become a part of another's misery? Where was the suffering to come in unless there was to be self-denial of some kind? That self-denial became apparent to them as they acted on their determination to share the deepest suffering and sin of the city.

They reasoned this way for themselves, not judging others. They were simply keeping their own pledge to do as Jesus would do, as they honestly judged He would do in their place. That was what they had promised. They would not quarrel with the results.

The Bishop had money of his own. Everyone who knew him knew that he was worth a small fortune. Dr. Bruce had acquired and saved more than a comfortable savings of his own through his literary endeavors. The two friends agreed at once to put the bulk of their combined worth into the work, most of it into the furnishing of the Settlement House.

CHAPTER 26

Nazareth Avenue Church was experiencing a revolution, an absolute spiritual renaissance—something never even believed possible in all its history. The simple appeal to do as Jesus would do had created astonishing repercussions. The response to that appeal was very much the same as in Henry Maxwell's church in Raymond, only this church was far more aristocratic, wealthy, and set in its ways.

Adding to the furor was the Sunday morning in early summer when Pastor Bruce came to the pulpit and announced his resignation. His words took everyone—except the official church board—completely by surprise. The sanctuary was suddenly charged with silent questions. The news spread across the city almost immediately.

Public astonishment reached its height when it became known that the Bishop had also announced his resignation and retirement in order to live in the center of Chicago's crime-ridden and hopeless inner city.

"But why not?" the Bishop replied to one valued friend who had almost with tears tried to dissuade him from his purpose. "Why should what the Bruces and I plan to do seem like such a remarkable thing, as if it were unheard of that a doctor of Divinity and a Bishop should want to save lost souls in this particular manner? Ministers and lay people have been doing this for hundreds of years. If we were resigning our positions for the purpose of going to Calcutta, the slums of Brazil, or any place in Africa, the churches and their people would remark on the heroism of missions. Why should it seem so great a thing that we have been led to give our lives to help rescue the lost of our own city? Is it so unbelievable that two Christian ministers should be not only willing but eager to live close to the suffering in the world in order to know it and share it? Is it such a rare thing that my love for humanity should take this particular form of expression in the salvation of the whole person?"

Even though the Bishop and the Bruces had been able to convince themselves that there was nothing so remarkable about their decision, the world outside their churches continued to talk and express their astonishment. How could two men, so prominent in Christian ministry, leave their comfortable homes, voluntarily resign their comfortable positions, and begin a life of suffering and hardship? Is such a radical move necessary for those who walk in His steps?

Nazareth Avenue Church said "good-bye" to its pastor and his wife for the most part with regret, although there was a sense of relief on the part of those who had refused to take the pledge. Dr. Bruce carried with him the respect of businessmen and women who realized that such a move in their own careers would have meant ruin. They carried a genuine admiration for his courage and consistency in their hearts. These business people had known the minister many years as a kindly, conservative, consistent man, but the thought of him sacrificing his family and career in this way was unbelievable to them. In fairness, when they understood the burden that was on his heart, they gave their pastor credit for being consistent with his conviction concerning the true meaning of following Jesus.

Some in Nazareth Avenue Church never understood Dr. Bruce's reasoning. The good news is that the church never lost the momentum of the discipleship movement Dr. Bruce had begun.

It was fall again, and the city was facing another hard winter. On one particular afternoon in autumn, the Bishop stood on the front stoop of the Settlement House looking at the squalid world for which God was making he and his brother, Calvin Bruce, at least partially responsible. Theirs was a tough responsibility to shake, even for a brief hour of rest and relaxation. Stepping onto the sidewalk, the Bishop began a purposeful stroll around the neighborhood. He intended to stop by and visit a new friend a few blocks over. Cars were of little use within the neighborhood; there was never parking and the constant threat of theft. Besides, there seemed to be something primitive and basic about being on foot—so the Bishop usually walked. On this particular fall day, he found himself on a new street, and almost immediately he found himself attracted to a shop that looked different from the others.

The place that attracted his notice was a small house next to an automatic laundry. The cleanliness of the front windows and sidewalk was remarkable in itself. Inside the window, there was a tempting display of baked goods with prices attached. The unique shop filled him with a sense of persistent curiosity. As he stood looking at the window display, the shop door opened and Felicia Sterling emerged.

"Felicia!" exclaimed the Bishop. "When did you move back to Chicago and into my new parish without my knowledge?"

"How did you find me so soon?" inquired Felicia.

"Why, don't you know? These are the only clean windows on the block."

"I believe they are," replied Felicia with a laugh that did the Bishop good.

"But why have you come to Chicago without telling me?" asked the Bishop, seeing in her a reminder of the sophisticated world he used to know. A world he had no desire to return to.

"Well, my dear Bishop," said Felicia, who had always looked to him as a father figure, and not a church administrator. "I knew how overwhelmed you were with your work. I did not want to burden you with my plans. And besides, I am going to offer you my services. I planned to drop by in a few days and ask for your advice. I am settled here for the present in three rooms behind the shop. One of Rachel Winslow's music students is living with me and helping out in the shop. Her name is Martha. She is currently taking a course in violin from Virginia Page. It's a small world after all, wouldn't you agree?" Felicia looked a bit overwhelmed. "I have begun an experiment in diet and food management for the poor. I may be an expert in the food part of my ministry, but I also want to use my business to reach hearts. That's where I need your help, dear Bishop."

"You tell me what I can do to help," he replied, catching Felicia's spirit and sense of purpose.

"Martha can help you out with the music at the Settlement House. Her violin should be a nice addition. And, I would love to help out with the cooking. The truth is that I had planned to get settled and organize myself and then come to you with some real skill to offer. I'll be fortunate to earn a living at this point."

"I'm sure you will do well." the Bishop said a little doubtfully. "What are those things?"

"Those things!" said Felicia indignantly. "I will have you know, sir, that 'those things' are the best-cooked, purest baked goods in this entire city."

"I don't doubt it," the Bishop replied hastily, his eyes twinkling. "Still, the proof is in the pudding . . . well, you know what I mean."

"Come on in and try some!" she exclaimed. "You look as if you haven't had a good meal for a month."

She insisted he come and meet Martha, a bright-eyed girl with short, curly hair and an unmistakable musical talent.

"Go right on practicing, Martha. This is the Bishop. You've heard me speak of him often." Martha nodded. Felicia turned to the Bishop, "Here, sit down and try these sweeties."

In just a few minutes, Felicia had bustled back and forth between the little store and the sitting room. She collected enough samples for an improvised but well-balanced lunch, upon which the Bishop feasted. He was thoroughly delighted by this unexpected discovery of an old friend with a distinct talent for baking—not to mention the promise of excellent ministry days ahead.

"I thought you'd at least say it is as good as the church potluck dinners you used to endure," laughed Felicia. "Actually, this meal was prepared on what could be purchased with a few food stamps."

"As good as! Never. This surpasses any tuna casserole and three bean salad, Felicia. But you must come to the Settlement House. I want you to see what we're doing. From this short conversation,

I'm beginning to see what your plan might be. You have so much to contribute to our Settlement House ministry. I suppose you plan to continue living here and teaching the value of healthy living and eating. Right?"

"Indeed I do," Felicia answered earnestly. "That is my calling."

"Absolutely! Thank God for your sense of mission. When I pulled out of my other world," the Bishop smiled at the phrase, "they were talking a good deal about the 'new woman.' If you are one of them, I am a convert right here and now."

"Flattery! Is there no escape from it, even in the slums of Chicago?" Felicia laughed again.

Felicia wanted to visit the Settlement House, so she decided to walk back with him and demand a tour. She was amazed at the results of what considerable money, good planning, and a great deal of consecrated effort had accomplished. They walked through the building talking incessantly. She was the embodiment of enthusiasm.

In the basement, Felicia heard the unmistakable sound of carpentry tools. The Bishop pushed open the door to a small but well-equipped shop. A young man clad in jeans and a shirt and wearing a White Sox cap on his head was whistling and working a plane over a piece of wood. He looked up as the two entered, and took off his cap. As he did so, his little finger carried a small curled shaving up to his hair and caught it there.

"Felicia Sterling, Stephen Clyde," said the Bishop. "Steve is one of our volunteers. He's here two afternoons a week."

Just then the Bishop was called upstairs and excused himself for a moment, leaving Felicia and the young carpenter alone.

"We've met before," said Felicia studying him intently. She offered her hand for a shake, and he took it with obvious pleasure.

"Yes, 'back in the other world,' as the Bishop says," replied the young man.

"Yes." Felicia hesitated. "I am very glad to see you again."

"Are you?" A flush of pleasure found its way to Clyde's forehead. "You have had a great deal of trouble since—since—then," he said, and then he was afraid he had hurt her or called up painful memories. But all of that was behind her.

"Yes, and you also. How is it that you're working here?"

"It is a long story, Felicia. My father lost his money and I was forced to fend for myself like all those other hardworking souls. A good thing for me. Matter of fact, the Bishop says I ought to be grateful for it. Truth is, I'm happier now than I have ever been. I learned a trade, and it's a good feeling to take responsibility for your own life. I am working as a night clerk at one of the downtown hotels. That Sunday morning when you took the pledge at Nazareth Avenue Church, I took it with you and the others."

"Did you?" said Felicia slowly. "I'm glad."

Just then the Bishop came back, and a few moments later, he and Felicia continued the tour leaving the young carpenter to his work. Someone noticed that he whistled louder than ever as he planed.

"Felicia," said the Bishop, "did you know Stephen Clyde before?"

"Yes, 'back in the world,' dear Bishop. He was one of my acquaintances at Nazareth Avenue Church."

"Ah!" said the Bishop. "What a lovely coincidence."

Felicia's face glowed for an instant. Then she looked her companion in the eyes frankly and said, "Really, Bishop!"

"I believe it would be just like God to bring you two across each other's paths at this time. After all," he said, like the sensible, good man that he was, "is not romance a part of our nature? Love is older than I am, and wiser!"

The week following, the Bishop had an experience that was very much a part of the Settlement House history. He was walking back to the House very late one night after a labor negotiating meeting when two men jumped out from behind an old fence that shut off an abandoned factory from the street. One of the men thrust a pistol in his face, and the other threatened him with a knife.

"Put your hands against this wall, and be quick about it!" said the one with the gun.

The place was solitary—there wasn't another person on the street. The Bishop had no thought of resistance. He did as the young men demanded, trying to stay calm as they went through his pockets. Standing there with his hands in the air, an ignorant spectator might have thought that he was praying for the souls of these two men—and so he was. Remarkably, that prayer was clearly answered that very night.

CHAPTER 27

Righteousness goes before him and
prepares the way for his steps.
Psalm 85:13

The Bishop was not in the habit of carrying much money with him, causing the man with the knife to curse at the small amount he found. The thug with the pistol motioned to his watch. "Might as well get all we can outta this job!"

Suddenly the two men heard the sound of footsteps coming toward them.

"Get him behind the fence! We haven't finished with him yet! Keep your mouth shut if you know . . . ," the man with the pistol demanded.

The man with the pistol made a significant gesture with it and, with his companion, pulled and pushed the Bishop down the alley and through an opening in the fence. The three stood still in the shadows until the footsteps passed.

"Now, then, have you got the watch?" asked the man with the pistol.

"No, I was just gettin' to that. . . ."

"Then get it!"

"No, don't take it," the Bishop argued. "It was a gift from a very dear friend. I would hate to lose it."

At the sound of the Bishop's voice, the man with the pistol stared as if he had suddenly been shot by his own weapon. With a quick movement of his other hand, he turned the Bishop's head toward what little light was shining from the alleyway, at the same time taking a step nearer. Then, to the amazement of his companion, he said roughly:

"Leave the watch alone! We've got the money. That's enough!"

"Enough? Five dollars, maybe! You don't think—"

Before the man with the knife could say another word he was confronted with the muzzle of the pistol turned from the Bishop's head toward his own.

"Leave the watch! And put back the money too. This is the Bishop—the Bishop—do you hear?"

"Hey, who gives a . . . ?"

"I said put the money back, or I'll blow a hole through your head that'll let in more sense than you have to spare now!" said the other.

For a second, the man with the knife hesitated at this strange turn of events. Then he hastily dropped the money back into the rifled pocket.

"You can take your hands down, sir." The man said with rough respect as he lowered his weapon. He still kept his eye on the other man. The Bishop carefully brought his arms to his side, and looked earnestly at the two men. In the dim light, it was difficult to distinguish features. He was evidently free to go his way now, but he stood there and did not move.

"You can go. There's no reason to stay on our account." The man who had acted as spokesman turned and sat down on an empty barrel. The other man stood viciously digging his knife into the wooden fence.

"That's just what I am staying for," replied the Bishop. He sat down on a upside-down trash barrel.

"You must like our company. Never knew anyone who enjoyed our company so much," declared the man standing. He laughed sarcastically.

"Shut up!" exclaimed the other. "We don't need your company on this road to hell."

"I wish you'd let me help you," the Bishop said gently. After a moment of silence, he spoke slowly like one who had finally decided upon a plan he had at first rejected.

"Do you remember ever seeing me before?"

"No," replied the Bishop, squinting to get a better look at his face. "The light is not very good, and I really can't get a good look at you."

"Do you know me now?" the man suddenly pulled back his sweatshirt hood and came so close to the Bishop that they were near enough to touch each other.

The minute the Bishop saw him up close, a long-past memory stirred in him. The man helped him out.

"Don't you remember one day back in '81 or '82 a man came to your house and told a story about his wife and child having been burned to death in a tenement fire in New York?"

"Yes, I remember now." The other man seemed to be interested. He stopped fidgeting with his knife and listened.

"You took me into your house that night and spent all the next day trying to find me a job. You found me a job in a warehouse, and I promised to give up crack."

"I remember it now. I hope you have kept your promise."

The man laughed savagely. Then he struck his hand against the fence with such sudden passion that he drew blood.

"Kept it! I was high within a week! I've been snorting ever since. But I've never forgotten you or your prayer. Do you remember the morning after I came to your house? After breakfast, you had prayer and asked me to come in and sit with the others. That really got to me! My mother used to pray—next to my bed when I was a kid. I never forgot your prayer that morning. You prayed for me just like my mother used to. You didn't seem to care how I looked or smelled or the fact that I was more than half drunk when I rang your doorbell."

The Bishop tried to put a hand on the man's shoulder, but he shrugged it off.

"Nah, you shouldn't touch me. I'm filthy. But know what . . . ?"

The Bishop shook his head.

"I'll tell you what, that prayer of yours stuck to me. Even though I broke my promise not to use drugs into a thousand pieces; even though I lost the job you found me—I never forgot you or your prayer. I don't know what good it has done me, but I never forgot it. And I won't do any harm to you or let anyone else harm you. So you're free to go. That's my reason."

The Bishop did not stir. Somewhere a church clock struck one. The man put on his cap and went back over to his friend. The Bishop was thinking hard.

"How long is it since you've had a job?"

"More'n six months since either of us did anything—unless you count 'holding up' people. I call it a pretty stressful kind of job myself, especially when we put in a night like this and don't make nothin'."

"Suppose I found good jobs for both of you? Would you quit this and begin all over?"

What's the use?" the man with the pistol spoke sullenly. "I've reformed a hundred times. Every time I go down deeper. Hell's already foreclosed on me. It's too late."

"No!" retorted the Bishop. Never had he stood before an audience and felt such a longing to see a soul redeemed as he did this very moment. All the time he sat there on the trash can, he prayed, *Oh, Lord Jesus, give me the souls of these two for You!*

"No!" the Bishop repeated. "What does God want of you two men? It doesn't so much matter what I want. But in this case He wants exactly what I want. You two men are of infinite value to Him."

And then his strong memory shifted into operation and came to his aid. He remembered the man's name in spite of the years that lay between his coming to the house and the present moment.

"Phillip Burns," he said, "if you and your friend here will go home with me tonight, I will find you both honorable jobs. I will believe in you and trust you. You're both young men. Why should God lose you? It's a great thing to know the love of the Great Father. It is a small thing that I should care for you. But if you need to be reminded that there is love in the world, please credit my concern for you as genuine Christian love. Make another try at it, God will help you."

"But what about . . .?" both men sputtered at once.

Reading their thoughts, the Bishop went on, "No one but God and you and myself will ever know what took place here tonight. Come! We'll fight it out together, you two and me."

At that point, the Bishop prayed directly for the souls of the two men. Before long Burns was sobbing with his face in his hands. The other man was harder to move, and without a previous knowledge of the Bishop, tried to ignore the prayer and Burns. But as the prayer went on, he too responded to the power of the Holy Spirit that permeated the alley.

It is no exaggeration to say that the same supernatural presence that smote Paul on the road to Damascus, and poured through Henry Maxwell's church, and had again broken irresistibly over the Nazareth Avenue congregation, was now manifested in God's presence in this forsaken corner of Chicago. The prayer seemed to break open the self-made crust that for years had surrounded them and shut them off from divine communication. It was a startling revelation for both men.

When the Bishop stopped praying, he looked up and discovered that Burns was still sitting with his head bowed between his knees. The man leaning against the fence looked at the Bishop with a new expression of awe, repentance, and astonishment; and a gleam of joy struggled for expression. The Bishop rose.

"Come, my brothers. God is good. You will stay at the Settlement House tonight, and I will make good on my promise about work."

The two men followed him in silence. When they reached the House, it was after two o'clock. He let them in and showed them to a room. Then, he paused for a moment at the door. His tall, commanding figure in the doorway and his pale face, worn with his recent experience, was illuminated with a divine glory.

"God bless you, my brothers!" he said, and leaving them his benediction, he went away.

In the morning, he almost dreaded to face the men. But the changes from the night before had not worn away. True to his promise, he found work for both of them. The janitor at the Settlement needed an assistant, owing to the growth of the work there. So Burns was given the job. The Bishop succeeded in getting his companion a position as a driver for a firm of warehouse drapery manufacturers not far from Settlement House. And the Holy Spirit began His marvelous work of regeneration in these two dark, sinful men.

CHAPTER 28

It was the afternoon of the day Burns began his new job as assistant janitor. One of his daily tasks was to keep the property picked up around the steps and sidewalks of Settlement House. That is precisely what he was doing when suddenly he spied his drug supplier standing at the curb smiling at him. Burns looked away quickly, but the pusher was still there when he glanced that direction again. The tall skinny dealer grinned sardonically and called out, "Hey Burns, ya ain't kickin' the habit are ya?"

Phil looked away again. This time his eyes were caught by a bar sign right across the street. There was another one next to that, and a third one in the next block. All of them seemed to beckon him.

"What'sa matter, Burns? Please tell me; you gettin' religion?"

Burns looked up at his nemeses, then straightened himself up, and called back, "I'm thinkin' religion's got me, that's what I'm thinkin.'"

The janitor took a tighter grip on his broom, and with great determination, continued to sweep the stoop and front walk, ignoring the dealer. When he looked up again, the man was gone.

"Oh, God!" he whispered under his breath. The Bishop and Dr. Bruce were at a neighborhood meeting in an apartment complex somewhere in the area, but Burns didn't know exactly where. His face was pale with fear and the agony of his conflict. Gradually, he edged out again toward the stoop and stepped down.

He was on the sidewalk now. By degrees, he seemed to be pulled toward the nearest bar. He imagined he could smell the beer and booze. To this man struggling to free himself from the grip of alcohol, those odors seemed like the infernal sulfur of the lowest hell, dragging him closer to the source.

Before he could comprehend what was happening, Burns found himself on the wrong side of the street, facing the front of the bar and staring inside as if he were in a trance. Maybe it was his imagination, but he could swear the tall skinny dealer was standing in the doorway beckoning for him to come in and enjoy what was inside. Phil Burns felt his mouth and throat go dry, as he took another step toward the bar. The beckoning figure with the devilish smile was still in the doorway. Burns took one more step toward the door. He reached out to push open the door, just as a tall figure rounded the corner. It was the Bishop.

He seized Burns by the arm and despite his protests marched him back across the street. The frenzied man, now desperate, shrieked out an oath and struck out savagely at his friend. It is doubtful if he really knew at first who was snatching him away from the door. The blow fell upon the Bishop's face and tore a gash in his cheek, but he never so much as uttered a word. Instead, he felt a deep emotion sweep over him. He picked Burns up as if he were a child and literally carried him up the steps and into the house. He put him down in the hall and then shut the door and leaned against it.

Burns fell to the floor sobbing, and the Bishop knelt beside him, moved with unspeakable pity for the man's struggle.

"Pray, Burns—pray as you never prayed before! Nothing else will help you!"

"Oh, God! Pray with me, Bishop! Oh, God, help me! Save me from myself!" cried Burns. The Bishop placed his arm around the young man's shoulder and prayed with him.

After the last "amen," Burns went to his room. When he reappeared that evening, he was like a humble child, and the Bishop went his way wiser from the experience. He had learned something about the awful power of addiction over the lives of its victims and something more about what it means to walk in the steps of Jesus.

The bars and the drug dealers were still everywhere Burns looked. They lined the streets of the district like so many set traps. How long would he be able to resist the temptation? The Bishop noticed for the first time that the air of the whole district seemed to be impregnated with the smell of alcohol. "How long, O Lord, how long?" he prayed. Calvin Bruce, hearing the Bishop talking to himself about the situation, came out, and the two friends discussed Burns and his struggle.

"Did you ever make any inquiries about who owns the property next door?" asked the Bishop.

"No, I haven't taken the time to do it. I will though, if you think it would be worthwhile. But, Edward, what can we do? We can't clean up the entire city single-handedly. Alcohol and drugs have a powerful hold on our nation, and the churches and government seem powerless to change it."

"God will help us to overcome in time," was the reply. "Meanwhile, I think we have a right to know who controls these bars and drug houses so near the Settlement House."

"I'll find out," promised Dr. Bruce.

Two days later, he walked into the office of a Chicago businessman, whom he knew to be a member of Nazareth Avenue Church. Dr. Bruce introduced himself to the receptionist and asked to see him. He was cordially received by his old parishioner, who welcomed him into his office and encouraged him to take all the time he wanted.

"I want to know about the property adjacent to the Settlement House, where the Bishop and I are now ministering. I'm going to speak plainly, because life is too short and too serious for us both to have any foolish hesitation about this matter. Clayton, do you think it is right to rent that property for a bar and let drug houses go unchallenged? I always considered you to be the epitome of above-board business activities in this city."

Dr. Bruce's question was direct and uncompromising. The effect on his old parishioner was instantaneous.

Hot blood mounted to the man's face. Then he grew pale and dropped his head into his hands.

When he looked up again, Dr. Bruce was amazed to see a look of agony cross his face.

"Doctor, did you know that I took the discipleship pledge that morning with the others?"

"Yes, I remember."

"But you don't know how I have struggled to keep that promise. I have been tormented by my failure, and I suppose I finally just gave up. That property has been Satan's great bargaining chip. You see, inexplicably I found that all my other properties seemed to be failing, while this particular piece began to pay better than ever before. I knew perfectly well that Jesus would never allow his property to be used for such a purpose. There is no need for you to say another word, Dr. Bruce. I have been in agony for some time, trying to come to grips with the fact that I would let earthly gain keep me from keeping my promise to follow my Savior."

Clayton held out his hand to Dr. Bruce, who took it kindly and shook it with conviction. Before parting, the minister declared, "You are assisting God in tearing down a wall of temptation to one very specific individual, as well as for so many others in that tormented part of Chicago."

Clayton's struggle was just a part of Nazareth Avenue Church's history since that memorable morning when the Holy Spirit blessed this holy pledge. The Spirit was brooding over the city with a mighty eagerness, waiting for the disciples to stand up to the call of sacrifice and suffering. He was beginning to touch hearts that had become dull and cold, and challenge the financial giants of the city who were immersed in their ungodly battle to control wealth at all costs. He was stirring the church as never before. The Bishop and Dr. Bruce had already seen miracles in their ministry at the Settlement House, but they were soon to see far greater things than they had ever imagined. There would be more astonishing revelations of divine power than they had supposed possible in this present age.

Within a month, the bar and drug houses near the Settlement House were closed. Clayton chose not to renew the lease for the bar and had the abandoned drug houses leveled. In an act of genuine repentance, he then offered the remaining buildings to the Bishop and Dr. Bruce for new Settlement House projects. The ministry had grown so quickly that the original building was no longer sufficient.

High on the list of important ministries for the Settlement House, was the nutrition center suggested by Felicia. It was not a month after Clayton turned the bar property over to the Settlement that Felicia found herself working to persuade the Bishop and Dr. Bruce that a model kitchen and classroom could be set up in what had been the bar and dance floor.

"Felicia, the time has come for you to tell us your plan in full," said the Bishop one evening as he, Dr. and Mrs. Bruce, and Felicia were checking out the other buildings on the property.

"Well, I have long thought that we could train some of our women to work as Christian domestics," enthused Felicia with an air of wisdom that made Mrs. Bruce smile, recognizing the transformation this young woman had experienced. "And I have reached certain conclusions that I doubt you men will be able to understand, though Mrs. Bruce will certainly understand."

"We know we are novices, Felicia. Go on," said the Bishop with a twinkle.

"Then this is what I propose to do. The old bar building is large enough to be remodeled into a suite of rooms that could be patterned after an ordinary house. My plan is to teach housekeeping and cooking to women who will afterwards go out to work in private homes. The course will be six months in length, and during that time, I will teach basic cooking and housekeeping skills, while endeavoring to instill a love for God and an appreciation for quality work."

"Hold on, Felicia!" the Bishop interrupted, "this is not the age of miracles!"

"Then we will make it one," replied Felicia. "I already know plenty of women who could be helped by such a project. I am excited because I have seen what a difference the nutrition center has made in the lives of many poor inner-city families.

"Felicia, if you can accomplish half what you propose, this community will be blessed," said Mrs. Bruce. "It won't be easy, especially with all your other projects, but I say, God bless you as you try."

"So say we all!" declared Dr. Bruce and the Bishop, and from that evening on, Felicia plunged headlong into her new endeavor.

It must be said that Felicia's plan succeeded beyond all expectations. She developed wonderful powers of persuasion, and taught her girls with astonishing rapidity to perform all sorts of housework and cook with style. In time, the graduates of Felicia's housekeeping and cooking school came to be prized employees across the city.

During the depth of winter, newspapers and local television stations reported on the marked contrast between the city's "haves" and "have-nots." For too many, the bitter struggle for food and shelter made the winter months unbearable. At the same time, wealthy Chicagoans thought of winter as the festive time of year. Never had there been such a succession of parties, receptions, and formal dinners. The opera and the theater had never before been so crowded with fashionable audiences. Never had there been such a lavish display of wealth and finery.

On the other hand, never had the deep want and suffering been so cruel, sharp, and desperate for those who struggled to provide the very necessities of life. Never had the winds blowing off the lake been so chilling and so effectively penetrated the thin walls of the homes in the tenement buildings in the Settlement House neighborhood. Night after night, the Bishop and Dr. Bruce with their volunteers went out and rescued men and women and children from the suffering of physical need. Vast quantities of food and clothing and large sums of money were donated by churches and other charitable organizations, but the personal touch of Christian discipleship was more difficult to secure on a week-to-week basis.

Volunteers to help with distribution were few, and it was anyone's guess where the pledged disciples were. Why weren't they obeying the Master's command to go to the suffering in order to diminish their physical need and tell them of God's constant love? The Bishop found his heart sink within him as he faced this fact more than any other. Individuals would give quantities of money, but nothing of their own time and effort. The money that most gave did not represent any real sacrifice. They gave in a way that hurt them the least. Where was the sacrifice of those who had pledged to follow Jesus? Dr. Bruce was appalled to discover how few men and women in the churches were willing to suffer any genuine inconvenience for the sake of the less fortunate among them.

Could it be that charity is no more than the surrendering of worn-out clothing or a $10 bill handed to some stranger to aid a benevolent organization? Can real charity be so impersonal and convenient? Are we to love and care for only those in our closest circle of friends and family and turn an ear of indifference to the disagreeable who pass through our lives?

All these questions plagued the Bishop as he plunged deeper into the sorrow and suffering of that bitter winter. While he was bearing his cross with joy; silently, powerfully, and continually, the Holy Spirit was moving through the churches— even the aristocratic, wealthy, ease-loving churches whose members shunned the misery of the poor as they would shun a contagious disease.

This fact was recognized by the Settlement House workers in a startling way one morning. Perhaps no incident of that winter shows more clearly the momentum of Dr. Bruce and the Bishop's commitment to do as Jesus would do.

CHAPTER 29

Breakfast at the Settlement House was the one hour in the day when the whole family was able to be together for a meal and a few moments of relaxation. There was a great deal of good-natured banter and fun. The Bishop told his best stories, and Dr. Bruce was at his best with his own anecdotes. This company of disciples was in a good humor in spite of the spirit of hardships that dogged their steps daily. In fact, the Bishop often said the gift of humor was as God-given as any other, and in his own case it often served as his safety valve.

This particular morning, he was reading aloud from the morning paper. Suddenly he paused and his face grew stern and sad. Those sitting around the table were startled by the change in his countenance and a hush fell over the table.

". . . shot and killed while stealing old sticks of lumber from a building site. The man had been unemployed for six months and there was no heat in the house except for a woodburning fireplace. The family of eight was packed into a freezing three-room rental house on Chicago's west side."

The Bishop read these exact words right off the front page. He then read the detailed account of the shooting by security guards and the visit of the reporter to the house where the family lived. When he finished, there was complete silence in the room. The humor of the hour was swept away by this description of human tragedy. The current of human suffering flowed in a rushing stream past the Settlement House, dragging with it thousands who were on the verge of being pulled under by unemployment, addiction, and a lack of God.

There were various reactions to the news story. One of the newcomers, a young man preparing for the ministry, asked:

"Why didn't the man go to a government agency or a church and ask for help? I can't believe that Christian people who live in this city would knowingly allow anyone to go without food or heat."

"No, I don't believe Christians would intentionally do that," replied Dr. Bruce. "But we don't know what there is to know about this man. He may have been forced to ask for help so often before that, finally, in a moment of desperation, he determined to cut out the middle man and help himself. I have heard of such cases this winter."

"That's not the worst part of this tragedy," said the Bishop. "The awful thing about it is the fact that this man had been without work for six months."

"Why don't such people move somewhere else?" the seminary student asked naively.

"Or why not round up all the homeless and let the federal government supply jobs—like they did back in the thirties?" someone else suggested.

Dr. Bruce shook his head. How well he remembered his parents' accounts of those frightening days in the thirties. He could remember them talking about the bank crash and the long lines of unemployed standing outside factories. He also had a distant memory of an uncle who took his life when he could not provide for his family. Finally he spoke, "There was probably more than one reason why this particular man was forced to steal—not the least of which was his desperate unemployment."

"Meanwhile there are the wife and children," said Mrs. Bruce. "How awful! Where did you say the family was living?"

"The paper says they were living on the west side in the 'Penrose district.' I believe Penrose himself owns half of the houses in that block.

They are among the worst in that part of the city. And Penrose is a church member."

"Yes, he belongs to the Nazareth Avenue Church," replied Dr. Bruce in an embarrassed voice.

The Bishop rose from the table fired with anger. He was on the verge of condemning the man, when the doorbell rang and one of the residents went to the door. The group in the dining room caught their breath when they heard . . .

"Tell Dr. Bruce and the Bishop I must see them. Penrose is the name—Clarence Penrose. Dr. Bruce knows me."

The Bishop exchanged a significant look with Dr. Bruce, and the two men instantly left the table and went out into the hall.

"Come in, Mr. Penrose," said Dr. Bruce, and they ushered the visitor into a private room and closed the door.

Clarence Penrose was one of the best known men in Chicago. He came from an old family with great wealth and social distinction, and he had large property holdings in a half dozen parts of the city. He had been a member of Dr. Bruce's church for many years. He faced the two ministers with a look of agitation that indicated he was in the throes of some unusual anguish. He trembled as he spoke. Clarence Penrose had never before given in to such a strange emotion.

"Is it possible that you have heard about the shooting which took place last evening? The family lived in one of my houses. It is a terrible ... but that's not the primary cause for my visit." He stammered and looked anxiously into the two men's faces. The Bishop continued to look stern. *This man could have done a great deal to alleviate the horrors faced by those living in his properties,* he thought, *possibly he could have prevented this tragedy.*

Penrose turned toward Dr. Bruce. "Pastor!" he exclaimed with a note of terror in his voice. "I have come here to tell you that I have had an experience so unusual that nothing but the supernatural can explain it. You remember I was one of those who took the discipleship pledge to do as Jesus would do. I thought at the time, poor fool that I was, that I had all along been doing the Christian thing. I gave liberally to the church and various charities. But, I must tell you, I have been living in a perfect hell of contradictions ever since I took that pledge, Pastor. My daughter, Diana, took the pledge with me. She has been asking me a great many questions lately about the people who rent homes from us. 'Do we own any houses where poor people live? Do those people have what they need to survive the winter?' You know how a young person will ask questions like these.

"I went to bed with a very sour conscience. I could not sleep. In my head, I kept imagining that I was standing before the Judge on Judgment Day. He was asking me to give an account of my deeds here on earth. 'How many souls had I visited in prison? What had I done with my wealth?' Then He asked directly about my low-income housing; about the people who froze in winter and stifled in summer. 'Did I give any thought to them except to take their money? Would Jesus have done as I had done and was doing? Had I broken my pledge? How had I used my possessions? Had I used them to bless humanity, to relieve suffering, to bring joy to the distressed and hope to the despondent? I had received much. How much had I given?'"

Dr. Bruce and the Bishop glanced at each other. Neither could believe what they were hearing.

"All of this came to me in a vision while I was awake. I saw the Judge and heard him as distinctly as I see and hear you. I never saw the end of the vision. All I could see was the Judge pointing a condemning finger at me, and the rest was shut out by mist and darkness. I have not slept for twenty-four hours. The first thing I saw this morning was the account of the shooting at the construction site. I have not been able to shake off the horror and guilt."

Penrose paused suddenly. The two men looked at him solemnly. What power of the Holy Spirit moved the soul of this seemingly self-sufficient man? Suddenly into that room came a breath of cooling clean air similar to that which had swept over Henry Maxwell's church and through Nazareth Avenue. The Bishop laid his hand on Penrose's shoulder, and spoke, "My brother, God has been very near to you. Let us thank Him."

"Yes! Yes!" sobbed Penrose. He sat down at the table and covered his face with his hands. The Bishop prayed. Then Penrose quietly said: "Will you go with me to visit that family?" he pleaded.

That was the beginning of a new and unusual life for Clarence Penrose. From the moment he stepped into that wretched hovel of a home and faced for the first time in his life, a despair and suffering such as he had read of but did not know by personal contact, he was forever changed. In obedience to his pledge, Mr. Penrose began to do with his squalid rental properties as he knew Jesus would do.

Before the winds of winter reached their bitter climax, many more things occurred in the city which affected the lives of all the disciples who promised to walk in His steps.

One afternoon as Felicia came out of the Settlement House bound for the Penrose district to deliver food and clothing to several of the needy families there, Stephen Clyde opened the door of the basement carpentry shop just in time to meet her as she reached the sidewalk.

"Here, let me help you load that in your car, please," he said.

"You don't have to say 'please,' Stephen."

"I'd like to say something else," replied Stephen, surprised at his own boldness.

"Oh, really?" returned Felicia.

Stephen knew already that he loved Felicia. It had been a growing affection that began the first day she stepped into his shop.

"What else would you like to say, Stephen?" asked Felicia, not too innocently.

"Well . . . ," Stephen stalled, turning toward her, "I would like to say . . . 'Let me help you carry those boxes, my dear Felicia.'"

She turned to Stephen, almost afraid to reveal the love she felt for him, "Why don't you say it, then?"

"May I?" exclaimed Stephen, taking one of the boxes from her and brushing her hand in the process.

While no one but the two parties involved knew exactly when Stephen had proposed marriage to his Felicia, it was a red letter day around the Settlement House when the two were married. *For this cause,* [said the Lord Jesus Christ] *shall a man leave father and mother, and shall cleave to his wife* (Matthew 19:5 KJV). And Felicia and Stephen, united in their love for Christ and for each other, rendered deeper service than ever before to the ministry they had been called to.

Rachel Winslow came to Chicago for her cousin's wedding, and a few days later, she was joined there by Henry Maxwell, Virginia Page, Rollin Page, Alexander Powers, and President Marsh. The occasion was a remarkable gathering at the Settlement House in the main assembly hall. It had been arranged by the Bishop and Dr.

Bruce. It had taken some doing to persuade Reverend Maxwell and his fellow disciples in Raymond to come and be present at this meeting.

Invited to the Settlement Hall meeting that night were a great host of the homeless, men and women who could not support their families because there was no work. Some were on the verge of losing their faith in God and man. These motley citizens filled every chair the House could come up with. Some sat on the floor, but they were all eager to hear what the initiators of the meeting had to say. They were particularly anxious to hear from Henry Maxwell and the other disciples from Raymond.

That evening, the Holy Spirit moved across that packed Settlement House auditorium. Every man and woman present saw the Settlement motto over the door that asked the eternal question, "What would Jesus do?"

Henry Maxwell was touched with deep emotion as he looked up and saw the question. To think that all of this had come about because of a shabby young man who had spoken up in that long-ago morning service at the First Church of Raymond.

Was his great desire for all Christians to come together and ask this question going to be granted? Would the movement begun in Raymond actually spread throughout the country? He had come to Chicago with his friends partly to see if the answer to that question would be found here in the heart of the city. In a few minutes, he would face the people. He had grown very strong and calm since he first spoke with trembling to that company of working men and women in the steel mill, but now as then, he breathed a deeper prayer for help. Then he went in, and with the rest of the disciples, experienced one of the greatest and most important events of his life. Somehow he felt this meeting would bring him the answer to the next step in his constant determination to do what Jesus would do. And tonight, as he looked into the faces of the men and women who had for years been both strangers and enemies of the Church, his heart cried out: *"Oh, my Master, teach the Church, Your Church, how to follow in Your steps!"*

CHAPTER 30

Jesus answered, "If you want to be perfect,
go, sell your possessions and give to the poor,
and you will have treasure in heaven.
Then come, follow me."
Matthew 19:21

"Ladies and Gentlemen, the Reverend Henry Maxwell!"

Henry Maxwell strode to the podium and looked over the audience crowded into the Settlement Hall. It is doubtful that he had ever faced such an audience before. Not even the Rectangle district at its worst could provide such a cross section of men and women who had slipped out of the reach of the church and all Christian influence.

Pastor Maxwell's message was expressed in the simplest of words and concepts. It was filled with illustrations of men and women from Raymond who had been obedient to God. Every person in that audience knew something about Jesus Christ. They had some idea of His character, and however much they had grown bitter toward the forms of Christian hypocrisy or the social system, they preserved some standard of right and truth based upon the Person of Jesus.

So as Maxwell spoke, they responded with interest to the "What would Jesus do?" concept. He began to apply the question to social problems recognized by every person in the room, and faces all over the hall lit up with recognition when he touched on a familiar problem or attitude. Bodies leaned forward in their chairs, seemingly fascinated by the simplicity of Maxwell's message—and the way it was communicated to everyone present.

Over and over again, the preacher asked the question, "What would Jesus do?" and then applied it to the lifestyle of the common person. Finally, he turned it around and asked, "Suppose that were the motto not only of those in the churches but of the businessmen, politicians, newspaper publishers, blue-collar workers, and the wealthy and influential—how long would it take under such a standard of conduct to revolutionize the world?" Then Maxwell nailed his message down with this question, "What is the real trouble with our world? I would answer that we are suffering from selfishness. No one has ever lived who has succeeded in overcoming selfishness like Jesus. If men followed Him regardless of the outcome, the world would at once experience new life."

Maxwell had never experienced an audience like that. It seemed that that crowd of humanity, even in the midst of their own great need, were caught up in the workings of God. The Bishop and Dr. Bruce marveled at the unity they felt among this crowd of the sick and the bruised and the hated and the desperate. Perhaps they could honestly declare that Settlement House, with its varied programs and godly leaders, had somehow begun to bring a softening to the bitterness of men's hearts caused by neglect and indifference.

No one really knew what the individuals in that audience were experiencing within themselves. No one could guess at the pent-up feelings and resentment of the homeless and unemployed. There were women in the crowd who were known prostitutes; one man was known by Stephen to be a neighborhood drug pusher. Among those who had heard of the meeting and responded to an invitation to attend were twenty or thirty unemployed men who had strolled past the Settlement House that afternoon and read the notice of the meeting. They came out of curiosity mostly and to escape the bone-chilling east wind. It was a bitter night so the bars were full. In that whole section of Chicago with thousands of homes, there were pitifully few doors open to the "weary and heavy laden" of the streets as was the door of the Settlement House with its bright lights, sweet sound of music, and warmth of fellowship. There was the taste and smell of freshly baked cinnamon rolls and mugs of steaming coffee, and most of all, there was the Spirit of One who says, *Come unto Me.*

As had been the custom from the beginning at the Settlement House, an open discussion followed Reverend Maxwell's address. Presided over by the Bishop, any person in the hall was at liberty to ask questions, express opinions, or declare their convictions. After the Bishop explained the ground rules for discussion, a man near the middle of the hall immediately rose and began to speak.

"I want to say that what Reverend Maxwell has said tonight hits pretty close to home for me. I knew Jack Manning, the fellow he told about who died at his house. I worked as a typesetter with him in Philadelphia for two years. Jack was a good man. He loaned me five dollars once when I was in a hole, and I never got a chance to pay him back. He moved to New York, when computers took over the business, and I never saw him again.

Many of the men I know who were displaced by this new technology haven't had steady jobs since. People are fond of saying that progress is good, but you couldn't prove it by me. . . ." The Bishop started to stand, thinking the speaker was finished, but he started up again.

"About this Christianity stuff he preached about tonight, it's all right I guess, but how come I never see many church people suffering like we do? Except for a few people around here, I would say church people are just as selfish and greedy for money and success as the next guy."

Cries of "That's right!" and "That's the truth!" interrupted the speaker. The Bishop quieted the crowd as another man was coming to speak. He walked up to the podium and stood rather shyly and spoke:

"This is the first time I was ever in here, and maybe it'll be the last. Fact is, I am about at the end of my rope. I've been all over Chicago looking for decent, permanent work and I'm sick of it. I know I can't be the only one here that just feels fed up." There were sounds of general approval. Then the speaker brightened, "Say! I'd like to ask a question of the preacher, if that's OK."

"Fire away," replied Reverend Maxwell with a smile. "Of course, I can't promise an answer that will make you happy."

"This is my question." The man leaned forward and stretched out a long arm with a dramatic gesture. "I want to know what Jesus would do in my case. I've got a wife and three kids, whom I love deeply. It's hard to keep moving around, never able to settle anywhere so they can get set up in school. We've just been trying to get by on the money I was able to save from a construction job I finished a few months ago and government assistance. I want to stay put until my kids can finish the school year. I'm a carpenter by trade, and I've tried every way I know to get a job. You say we ought to take for our motto, 'What would Jesus do?' What would He do if He was out of work like me? I can't be someone else and ask the question. I want to work. Am I to blame because I can't manufacture a job for myself? I've got to live, and my wife and my kids have got to live. But how? 'What would Jesus do?' You say that's the question we ought to ask."

Reverend Maxwell sat by the podium staring at the great sea of faces all intently wondering how he would answer this man's question. Maxwell bowed his head for a moment. *Oh, God!* his heart prayed,

This is a tough question that brings up the entire issue of Your purposes for us. The situation this man raises is contrary to every desire You have for our welfare. Is there any condition more awful for a man in good health, who is able and eager to work and has an honest desire to take care of his family but cannot seem to find a job? What are the alternatives for such an individual? Must he accept assistance from the government or beg from his friends and family? "What would Jesus do?" It was a fair question for the man to ask. It was the only question he could ask, supposing him to be a disciple of Jesus. But what a question for any man to be obliged to answer under such conditions.

Henry Maxwell pondered this and much more. The Bishop sat with a look so serious and sad that it was not hard to tell how the question moved him. Dr. Bruce had his head bowed. The human problem had never before seemed to him so tragic as it had since he had taken the pledge and left his church to begin the Settlement House. "What would Jesus do?" It was a terrible question for someone in this man's situation. And still the man stood there, tall and gaunt and almost frightening in an appeal which grew more meaningful with each passing second. At length, Reverend Maxwell spoke.

"Is there any man in the room, who is a Christian disciple, who has been in this condition and has tried to do as Jesus would do? If so, such a man can answer this question better than I."

There was a moment's hush over the room and then a man near the front of the hall slowly rose. He was old, and the hand he laid on the back of the bench in front of him trembled slightly.

"I think I can safely say that many times I have been in the same condition as the man who just spoke. While I've always tried to be a Christian in all situations, I've not always asked this question, 'What would Jesus do?' when I've been out of work. But I do know I've always tried to be His disciple. Yes," the man went on, with a sad smile, "I've begged, and I've been to rescue missions, and government agencies, and soup kitchens run by various churches. I've done about everything at one time or another except steal and lie. I don't know as Jesus would have done some of the things I have been obliged to do for a living, but I know I have never knowingly done wrong when out of work. Sometimes I think maybe He would have starved sooner then beg. I don't know."

The old man's voice trembled and he looked around the room. When he sat down, a man who appeared to be a street worker sprang to his feet and poured out a torrent of abuse against big business. The minute his time was up a big, brawny fellow, who said he was a metal worker by trade, claimed the floor and declared that unions were the remedy for the problems they were facing.

Finally, the Bishop called "time" on the "free-for-all," and asked Rachel to sing.

Rachel Winslow had matured into a strong, even more beautiful Christian during the two years since she had first taken the pledge to do as Jesus would do, and her talent had been fully consecrated to the service of the Master. Before she sang at the Settlement House meeting, she prayed that God would touch hearts through her song. Her prayer was being answered as she sang.

Hark! The voice of Jesus calling,
Follow Me, follow Me!

While Rachel sang, a flood of memories poured over Henry Maxwell. He was reminded of his first experience at the storefront chapel in the Rectangle district, when Rachel sang the people into a state of calmness and reverence. The effect was the same here. Rachel's great natural ability would have made her a concert or opera singer in great demand. The men who drifted in from the street sat entranced by her voice.

The song poured through the hall as free and glad as if it were a foretaste of salvation itself. The older man who had spoken so sincerely absorbed the music with a deep love for what Rachel sang about. The man out of work who had wanted to know what Jesus would do in his place sat with one hand on the back of the bench in front of him and his great tragedy for the moment forgotten. The song, while it lasted, was food and work and warmth and union with his wife and babies once more. The man who had spoken so fiercely against the churches and ministers sat with his head erect, at first with a look of solid resistance, as if he stubbornly resisted introduction into any exercise even remotely connected with the church or its forms of worship. But gradually he yielded to the power that was swaying the hearts of all the persons in that room, and a look of sad thoughtfulness crept over his face.

The Bishop whispered to Dr. Bruce, "If the world could only hear the Gospel being preached through the lips of a consecrated communicator of God's love like Rachel, it would hasten the coming of the Kingdom more than any other one force."

Henry Maxwell shut his eyes while he listened to Rachel's solo. In his memory, he saw the chapel crowd in the Rectangle district. He longed to see the spread of new disciples coming out of Chicago. All that he was experiencing at the Settlement House burned into him a deeper belief that many of the city's problems could be solved if Christian citizens would follow Jesus as He commanded.

But what of this great mass of humanity—the ones sitting in the hall, neglected and desperate, the very type of people the Savior came to save, with all of their mistakes and wretchedness and loss of hope? That was what struck him most deeply. Did they turn their backs to Christ because the church had failed them? Was the church so far from the Master that the people no longer found Him there? Was it true that the church had lost its power and influence over the very people they had been called to minister to?

He was increasingly impressed with the appalling fact that comparatively few men in that hall, now being held quiet for a short time by Rachel's voice, represented thousands of others just like them, to whom a church and a minister were less of a source of comfort or happiness than a bar. Is that how it ought to be? How much were

Christians responsible for the human problem illustrated right in this hall tonight? Would the Christians of Chicago, like those of Raymond, be willing to walk in Jesus' steps so closely as to suffer—actually suffer—for His sake?

Henry Maxwell kept asking this question even after Rachel had finished singing and the meeting had come to an end. He asked it during and after an informal gathering with refreshments provided by Felicia's kitchen. He asked it while the company of Settlement House residents were having devotions with the Raymond visitors. He asked it during a conference with the Bishop and Dr. Bruce, which lasted until one o'clock. He asked it as he knelt again before sleeping and poured out his soul in a petition for spiritual baptism on the churches of North America such as they had never before known. He asked it the first thing in the morning and all through the day as he walked about in the Settlement House neighborhood among people so far removed from the life of Christ. *Would all the Christians in Chicago and around the country actually be willing to take up their crosses and follow Jesus?* This was the one question that continually demanded an answer.

CHAPTER 31

When he arrived in Chicago, his plan had been to return to Raymond in time to be in his own pulpit on Sunday. But Friday morning at the Settlement House, Henry Maxwell received a call from the pastor of one of the mega-churches in Chicago, requesting his presence in the pulpit for both the morning and evening services.

His first instinct was to refuse the invitation, but after prayerfully considering it, he accepted, believing the hand of God was in it. He would use this speaking opportunity as a way to further test his discipleship pledge. The occasion gave him a chance to prove the truth or falsehood of the severe charges made against the churches at the Settlement House meeting. How far would those church members go in self-denial for Jesus' sake? How closely would they be willing to walk in His steps? Would they be willing to suffer for Him?

Reverend Maxwell spent most of Saturday night praying. He had never experienced such a wrestling match in his soul, not even during his toughest testings in Raymond. Here in Chicago, the minister had found a new proving ground. The commitment of his own discipleship was receiving an added test and, at the same time, he was being led into greater truth.

Sunday morning, the incredibly huge church was filled to capacity. Coming onto the chancel platform after his all-night vigil, Henry Maxwell sensed the people's curiosity. They had heard of what transpired in Raymond, and how the discipleship movement had come out of what seemed to be a simple pledge. Besides the natural curiosity, there was something deeper, more serious present in the service. Reverend Maxwell felt it the moment he strode to the beautifully carved pulpit. With the knowledge that the Holy Spirit's presence was his strength, he opened his well-worn Bible, placed in on the pulpit, and bowed his head for a second of silent prayer.

Even though in the old days, he had considered himself to be a striking speaker, he realized that back then he had lacked the power and the resolve of a great persuader. But, he would hasten to add, ever since he had promised to do as Jesus would do, he had grown in a quality of persuasiveness that revealed a true eloquence. This morning, the congregation sensed the total sincerity of their guest and at the same time, were drawn by his humility. Here before them stood a man of God who had given himself to a goal that superceded success and public approval.

Without a note of conceit or self-aggrandizement, Maxwell reflected upon those dear people in Raymond who had taken the discipleship pledge to the glory of God. After attracting the audience's attention with personal stories, he turned to the Gospels and read the story of the young man who came to Jesus asking what he must do to obtain eternal life. He reminded his audience that Jesus tested the young man with the words, *Go, sell your possessions and give to the poor, and you will have treasure in heaven. Then come, follow me* (Matthew 19:21). But the young man was not willing to suffer to that extent. Like many of us today, he felt that if following Jesus meant suffering in that way, he was not willing. He would like to follow Jesus, but not if he had to give so much.

"Is it true?" continued Maxwell, his face glowing with an appealing passion that stirred the congregation. "Is it true?" he repeated "that many worshippers in today's Church would choose the action of the 'rich young ruler,' and refuse to follow Jesus because suffering and physical loss appeared to be a strong possibility? Are the Christians of this nation ready to have their discipleship tested? Are those with great resources ready to use those resources as Jesus would? How about the men and women with great talent? Are they ready to consecrate that talent to serve others as Jesus undoubtedly would do?

"Are we ready to take up the cross? Is it possible for membership of this church to sing with total honesty,

> *Jesus, I my cross have taken*
> *All to leave and follow Thee?*

"If we can sing those words in truth, then we may claim to be true disciples. But if our definition of being a Christian is simply the enjoyment of corporate worship; generosity with no personal sacrifice; good times surrounded by people we like and things we enjoy; living respectably and at the same time, avoiding the world's great masses of desperate and suffering humanity because it is too much pain to bear it— if this is our definition of Christianity, surely we are a long way from following the steps of Him Who carried His cross for us."

When Henry Maxwell finished his sermon, he paused and looked at the people with an expression they would never forget, but at that moment, did not understand. Packed into that fashionable church were hundreds of men and women who had for years lived the easy, satisfied life of nominal Christianity. During those moments, as the preacher stood and surveyed his listeners, a great silence fell over the congregation. In that silence every soul present became aware of the Divine Power—something they had never before experienced in that way.

Everyone expected the preacher to call for volunteers to take the pledge to do as Jesus would do, but Maxwell had been led by the Spirit to do otherwise. He delivered his message and then allowed the Spirit to do His work. He knew that the best results would come in this way.

He closed the morning service with a tender prayer that kept the congregation conscious of the divine presence lingering in that great auditorium. Slowly the people rose to leave, but many were stopped by a scene that was more than an emotional reaction to a good sermon.

Great numbers of men and women crowded around Reverend Maxwell to personally tell him of their promise to do as Jesus would do. It was a voluntary, spontaneous movement with results that could not yet be anticipated. To Maxwell, this was an answer to prayer that more than exceeded his greatest hopes.

In a prayer service that followed this outpouring, the Raymond experience was repeated. That evening, to Reverend Maxwell's joy, the church's youth group and its leaders came forward and solemnly took the pledge to do as Jesus would do. An indescribable spiritual wave broke over those who remained during the closing minutes of the meeting.

That Sunday was a remarkable day in the history of one of Chicago's influential mega-churches, but it was even more so in the history of the Reverend Henry Maxwell. When he was finally able to leave the church, he went directly to his room at the Settlement House and spent an hour with the Bishop and Dr. Bruce, joyously relating the wonderful events of the day.

One of Maxwell's rituals was to kneel for his final prayer of the day. While he was on his knees, he had a vision of what the world might be like when this new discipleship movement made its way into the conscience of all Christians. He was fully awake, but it seemed to him that he saw certain things with great clarity; partly as realities of the future, partly great longings that they might be realities. And this is what Henry Maxwell saw in this waking vision:

He saw himself, going back to Raymond First Church and living a much simpler lifestyle in a more self-denying fashion than he had yet been willing to live. In his vision, he saw ways in which he could help those who were dependent on him. He also saw, though more dimly, that the time would come when his position as pastor of the church would give him reason to suffer in greater ways, because of growing opposition to his radical interpretation of what he felt Jesus expected from His disciples. Through it all, he heard the words, *My grace is sufficient for you.* The vision continued.

He saw Rachel Winslow and Virginia Page continuing their work of service in the Rectangle district, and reaching out loving hands far beyond the limits of Raymond. He saw Rachel married to Rollin Page, both fully consecrated to the Master's use, both following His steps with an eagerness intensified and purified by their love for each other. And he heard Rachel's voice ringing out in slums and dark places of despair and sin, and drawing lost souls back to God and heaven.

He saw President Marsh of Lincoln College using his education and influence to purify the city, to inspire young men and women to lives of Christian service, always teaching them that education means great responsibility for helping the weak and the needy.

He saw Alexander Powers encountering serious family trials, with a constant sorrow due to the estrangement of wife and friends, but still honorable, and going his way serving the Master with all his strength—the Master whom he obeyed, even to the loss of his position and wealth.

He saw Milton Wright, the merchant, encountering business reversals and facing the future with vast business interests plunged in ruin through no fault of his own. But he also saw him coming out of those reversals with Christian integrity and beginning again to build a company that would be an example to hundreds of young people of what Jesus would do in business.

He saw Edward Norman, CEO of Norman Communications and publisher of the Raymond *Daily News*, creating an influential force in journalism that reflected Christian ideals and values, thanks to the money given by Virginia Page. The first of a series of such papers begun and carried on by other disciples who had also taken the pledge.

He saw Jasper Chase, who had denied his Master, growing into a cold, cynical, novelist, whose works were well received by critics, but constant reminders of his denial and the bitter remorse that, do what he would, no literary success could remove.

He saw Felicia and Stephen Clyde happily married, living a wonderful life together; joyful in suffering, pouring out their service into the dark, terrible places of the great city, and redeeming souls through the personal warmth of their home, dedicated to the homeless all about them.

He saw Dr. Bruce and the Bishop continuing their work at the Settlement House. He seemed to see the great blazing motto over the door enlarged and gleaming as if touched by the Master: *House ministry walked in the steps of Jesus.*

Henry Maxwell continued to pray, and his vision continued. Now the vision was more of a longing for what the future held. Would the Church of Jesus Christ in the city and throughout the country follow in the Master's footsteps? Was the movement begun in Raymond to have influence in but a few churches like Nazareth Avenue and the one where he had preached today, and then die out? Maxwell searched with agony for the vision again. Then he thought he saw the Church of Jesus begin to open its heart to the moving of the Spirit and rise up to the sacrifice of its ease and self-satisfaction in the name of Jesus. He thought he saw the motto, "What would Jesus do?" inscribed over every church door, and written on every church member's heart.

The vision vanished. Then it returned clearer than before, and he saw streams of young people from all over the world carrying in their great procession a banner on which was written, "What would Jesus do?" And he thought in the faces of the young men and women, he saw future joy in suffering, loss, self-denial, and martyrdom. And when this part of the vision slowly faded, he saw the figure of the Son of God beckoning to him and to all the other players in his life story. An angel choir somewhere was singing. There was a sound as of many voices and a shout as of a great victory. And the figure of Jesus grew more and more splendid. "Oh, Son of God, imprint upon this present age Your light and Your truth! Help us to follow Thee all the way!"

Henry Maxwell rose at last with the awe of one who has just seen heavenly things. He felt the human activity and the human sins of the world as never before. And with a hope that walks hand in hand with faith and love, Henry Maxwell, disciple of Jesus, laid himself down to sleep and dreamed of the regeneration of Christendom, and saw in his dream a Church of Jesus without spot or wrinkle or any such thing, following Christ all the way, walking obediently in His steps.

THE END

Steps to Peace with God

Step 1 | God's Purpose: Peace and Life

God loves you and wants you to experience peace and life—abundant and eternal.

The Bible Says . . .

". . . we have peace with God through our Lord Jesus Christ." Romans 5:1

"For God so loved the world that He gave His only begotten Son, that whoever believes in Him should not perish but have everlasting life." John 3:16

". . . I have come that they may have life, and that they may have it more abundantly." John 10:10b

Since God planned for us to have peace and the abundant life right now, why are most people not having this experience?

Step 2 | Our Problem: Separation

God created us in His own image to have an abundant life. He did not make us as robots to automatically love and obey Him, but gave us a will and a freedom of choice.

We chose to disobey God and go our own willful way. We still make this choice today. This results in separation from God.

Our choice results in separation from God.

The Bible Says . . .

"For all have sinned and fall short of the glory of God." Romans 3:23

"For the wages of sin is death, but the gift of God is eternal life in Christ Jesus our Lord." Romans 6:23

People (Sinful) God (Holy)

Our Attempts

There is only one remedy for this problem of separation.

Through the ages, individuals have tried in many ways to bridge this gap . . . without success . . .

The Bible Says . . .

"There is a way that seems right to man, but in the end it leads to death." Proverbs 14:12

"But your iniquities have separated you from God; and your sins have hidden His face from you, so that He will not hear." Isaiah 59:2

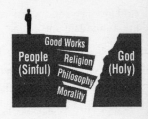

Step 3 God's Remedy: The Cross

Jesus Christ is the only answer to this problem. He died on the Cross and rose from the grave, paying the penalty for our sin and bridging the gap between God and people.

The Bible Says . . .

". . . God is on one side and all the people on the other side, and Christ Jesus, Himself man, is between them to bring them together . . ." 1 Timothy 2:5

"For Christ also has suffered once for sins, the just for the unjust, that He might bring us to God . . ." 1 Peter 3:18a

"But God demonstrates His own love for us in this: While we were still sinners, Christ died for us." Romans 5:8

God has provided the only way . . . we must make the choice . . .

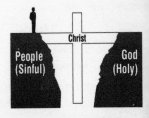

Step 4 | Our Response: Receive Christ

We must trust Jesus Christ and receive Him by personal invitation.

The Bible Says . . .

"Behold, I stand at the door and knock. If anyone hears My voice and opens the door, I will come in to him and dine with him, and he with Me." Revelation 3:20

"But as many as received Him, to them He gave the right to become children of God, even to those who believe in His name." John 1:12

". . . if you confess with your mouth the Lord Jesus and believe in your heart that God has raised Him from the dead, you will be saved." Romans 10:9

Are you here . . . or here?

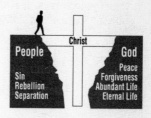

Is there any good reason why you cannot receive Jesus Christ right now?

How to receive Christ:

1. Admit your need (I am a sinner).
2. Be willing to turn from your sins (repent).
3. Believe that Jesus Christ died for you on the Cross and rose from the grave.
4. Through prayer, invite Jesus Christ to come in and control your life through the Holy Spirit. (Receive Him as Lord and Savior.)

What to Pray:

Dear Lord Jesus,

I know that I am a sinner and need Your forgiveness. I believe that You died for my sins. I want to turn from my sins. I now invite You to come into my heart and life. I want to trust and follow You as Lord and Savior.

In Jesus' name. Amen.

_____   _____
Date   Signature

God's Assurance: His Word

If you prayed this prayer,

The Bible Says...

"For 'whoever calls upon the name of the Lord will be saved.'"
Romans 10:13

Did you sincerely ask Jesus Christ to come into your life? Where is He right now? What has He given you?

"For it is by grace you have been saved, through faith—and this is not from yourselves, it is the gift of God—not by works, so that no one can boast." Ephesians 2:8,9

The Bible Says...

"He who has the Son has life; he who does not have the Son of God does not have life. These things I have written to you who believe in the name of the Son of God, that you may know that you have eternal life, and that you may continue to believe in the name of the Son of God." 1 John 5:12–13, NKJV

Receiving Christ, we are born into God's family through the supernatural work of the Holy Spirit who indwells every believer...this is called regeneration or the "new birth."

This is just the beginning of a wonderful new life in Christ. To deepen this relationship you should:

1. Read your Bible every day to know Christ better.
2. Talk to God in prayer every day.
3. Tell others about Christ.
4. Worship, fellowship, and serve with other Christians in a church where Christ is preached.
5. As Christ's representative in a needy world, demonstrate your new life by your love and concern for others.

God bless you as you do.

Billy Graham

If you want further help in the decision you have made, write to:
Billy Graham Evangelistic Association P.O. Box 779, Minneapolis, Minnesota 55440-0779